The Journal of the History of Philosophy Monograph Series
Edited by Richard A. Watson and Charles M. Young

Descartes on Seeing
Epistemology and Visual Perception

Celia Wolf-Devine

Published for
The Journal of the History of Philosophy, Inc.

SOUTHERN ILLINOIS UNIVERSITY PRESS
Carbondale and Edwardsville

Library of Congress Cataloging-in-Publication Data

Wolf-Devine, Celia, 1942–
    Descartes on seeing : epistemology and visual perception / Celia
Wolf-Devine.
        p.   cm. — (Journal of the history of philosophy monograph
    series)
    Includes bibliographical references and index.
    1. Descartes, René, 1596–1650—Contributions in concept of
perception.   2. Perception (Philosophy)—History—17th century.
I. Title. II. Series.
B1878.P47W6   1993
121'.3—dc20   92-12756
ISBN 0-8093-1838-5   CIP

Illustrations from *Oeuvres de Descartes*, ed. Charles Adam and Paul Tannery,
    1964–76, courtesy of Librairie Philosophique, J. Vrin, Paris.

The paper used in this publication meets the minimum requirements of
American National Standard for Information Sciences—Permanence
of Paper for Printed Library Materials, ANSI Z39.48-1984. ∞

CONTENTS

THE *JOURNAL OF THE HISTORY OF PHILOSOPHY*
Monograph Series

THE *JOURNAL OF THE HISTORY OF PHILOSOPHY* MONOGRAPH SERIES, CON-sisting of volumes averaging 80 to 120 pages, accommodates serious studies in the history of philosophy that are between article length and standard book size. Editors of learned journals have usually been able to publish such studies only by truncating them or by publishing them in sections. In this series, the *Journal of the History of Philosophy* presents, in volumes published by Southern Illinois University Press, such works in their entirety.

The historical range of the *Journal of the History of Philosophy* Monograph Series is the same as that of the *Journal* itself—from ancient Greek philosophy to the twentieth century. The series includes extended studies on given philosophers, ideas, and concepts; analyses of texts and controversies; new translations and commentaries on them; and new documentary findings about various thinkers and events in the history of philosophy.

The editors of the Monograph Series, the directors of the *Journal of the History of Philosophy,* and other qualified scholars evaluate submitted manuscripts. Those manuscripts concerning ancient and medieval philosophy should be sent to Professor Charles M. Young, Department of Philosophy, Claremont Graduate School, Claremont, CA 91711. Manuscripts on modern and recent philosophy should be sent to Professor Richard A. Watson, Department of Philosophy, Washington University, St. Louis, MO 63130. Manuscripts should be between 35,000 and 50,000 words in length and double-spaced throughout, including quotations, notes, and bibliography. Notes should be numbered separately for each chapter and placed in a section at the end of the manuscript.

Richard A. Watson
Charles M. Young
—Editors

ACKNOWLEDGMENTS

I THANK STONEHILL COLLEGE FOR SUMMER GRANT SUPPORT THAT ENABLED me to finish this monograph. I am also indebted to Owen Carroll of St. Mary's College for help with an earlier version; to Margaret Wilson who read the earlier version and suggested to me that I develop the material into a monograph; to Richard Watson for his excellent editorial suggestions; to an anonymous reader who encouraged me to include more material on late scholastic philosophy; to Andre Goddu who read and commented on this manuscript; to Tony Celano and Ralston Haynes for help with translations; to David Clemenson for some valuable discussions; and to my work-study student, Kimberly Giacapuzzi, for help with typing.

Finally, I am grateful to my husband, Phil Devine; without his help and encouragement, I would never have managed to finish it.

Descartes on Seeing

Introduction

THE MAIN FOCUS OF THIS ESSAY IS HISTORICAL. I CONSIDER HOW DESCARTES' theory of vision contributes to the victory of mechanistic natural philosophy over physical theories of a broadly Aristotelian sort and sets up a framework within which a whole new set of problems arises in the philosophy of perception. By Berkeley's time, for example, it is simply assumed that ideas are the immediate objects of perception, that colors have no existence outside the mind, and that a sharp distinction can be drawn between seeing and judging in vision. Descartes' theory of vision is very important to the genesis of all of these ideas—especially his understanding of the role of the retinal image in vision.

In addition to its historical significance, however, Descartes' theory of vision is also of value for anyone interested in the problems of mind/body dualism because in this theory Descartes grapples with what really happens in sensation more concretely and in more detail than he does anywhere else in his writings. Hence, Descartes' theory of vision exposes the points at which Cartesian dualism encounters difficulties with explaining perception. It is also a valuable case study showing a genuine two-way interaction between science and epistemology. Descartes' scientific account of perception has consequences for the scope and reliability of our knowledge of nature,[1] but philosophical considerations also sometimes influence him when he formulates hypotheses about the structure and functioning of the visual system.

The epistemological ramifications of Descartes' theory of perception as developed in his scientific writings and its connection with his more properly philosophical works have come under scrutiny recently by several scholars. Nancy Maull, for example, argues that the *Dioptrics (La Dioptrique)* is foundational to Descartes' scientific program in that it establishes the applicability of Euclidean geometry to nature.[2] And Ronald Arbini argues that Descartes' *Dioptrics* and related texts provide a "clear, coherent account of sense perception" intended "to solve the well known problems impugning 'external sense' perception advanced, but never resolved in his philosophical work,"[3] and he notes that the sorts of illusions Descartes cites in the First Meditation to discredit the senses involve distance, size, and shape perception—the very things he undertakes to explain in his optical writings.

Although I believe that Descartes' optical writings do shed light on epistemological issues arising elsewhere in his writings, they must be read as much as possible in light of his own intentions, and I do not find either Maull's or Arbini's accounts of these persuasive. Maull cites no textual evidence that Descartes was even aware of a need to prove that Euclidean geometry is applicable to nature (essentially Kant's problem), let alone that he envisioned the natural geometry theory as filling this gap in his system. And since the *Dioptrics* was written before the *Meditations (Meditationes de Prima Philosophiae)*, it seems unlikely that it was intended to resolve doubts left unresolved in the Sixth Meditation about distance, size, and shape perception. Besides, Descartes is far from suggesting that anything like certainty attaches to our visual spatial perception and indeed goes out of his way to stress the fact that all the means by which we perceive distance, situation, size, and shape are approximate and fallible. His own intentions are to explain visual perception mechanistically (by contrast with the Aristotelian way) and to develop his theories about light, refraction, lenses, etc., in ways that will be of practical use for improving our powers of vision.

Margaret Wilson examines Descartes' optical writings from a slightly different perspective in her attempt to shed light on the question of the extent to which he believes that sense perception enables us to perceive distinctly the determinate primary qualities of particular physical objects—say, the chair across the room. While she finds grounds for scepticism about this in many of Descartes' later writings, she finds evidence in the scientific writings and the Sixth Replies that we do perceive them distinctly but not by sense. The evidence is, however, not unambiguous, and she concludes that these texts are "far from presenting a coherent and consistent position, that can settle difficulties found in Descartes' remarks on the subject elsewhere."[4] I agree with Wilson that the scientific works on vision contain many problems and unresolved tensions, but I think that they make the best sense considered on their own first without our attempting to integrate them too closely with the Sixth Replies, since the fit between the former and the latter is not at all neat.

One problem of epistemological importance the optical writings do shed light on is the genesis of the idea that there exists a kind of sensory "given" that is immediately or directly seen and is different from the world as we normally experience it.[5] Descartes does not separate out what we "immediately" or directly see in quite the way later philosophers do, but his work contains the seeds of this sort of understanding of vision.

Connected with questions about the nature of the sensory "given" is the debate over whether or not Descartes' theory of perception is representationalist.[6] I do not address the issue of Descartes' alleged representationalism directly, since the meaning of the term *representationalism* is contested, and its use often obscures rather than clarifies the issues involved. Furthermore, there seem to be insuperable problems with such a theory, at least in its more clearly defined versions. Monte Cook, for example, says that a representational theory of perception goes beyond a merely causal theory (that our knowledge of the world is mediated by things such as retinal images and brain states) and holds that we perceive one thing by means of perceiving another distinct thing. We perceive external objects mediately by immediately perceiving retinal images, brain states, or some other "privileged sort of object."[7] So defined, however, representationalism fails because it involves a circularity and leads to a vicious regress. If I perceive X by means of perceiving Y, it must still be explained how I perceive Y; to explain perception we cannot invoke perception—the very thing we are trying to explain. In addition, perception requires sense organs. But with what sense organs do I perceive my retinal images or brain states? And would I not need other retinal images by means of which to see my retinal images—thus leading to an infinite regress?[8]

Although I take no position on whether Descartes is a representationalist, I believe that an analysis of his theory of vision provides insight into one of the main sources of the view that perception involves an inner object of some sort that mediates between the knower and the object known.[9] According to Descartes' metaphysics, such mediation takes place both because the mind (as subject) must confront the brain with the pattern of figures and motions present in it as an object and because his understanding of the role of the retinal image in vision leads him to suppose that the mind has some sort of access to the retinal image. Descartes, for the most part, avoids stating his theory in ways obviously vulnerable to the regress argument but only at the cost of leaving largely unexplained the way in which we have access to the retinal image (or its pineal correlate).

Before launching into a detailed consideration of Descartes' theory of vision, I shall set the stage by reflecting briefly on the reasons why the theory of vision is important both in the context of the debates of the seventeenth century and in more general terms. Human beings are creatures whose relationship with the physical world is largely regulated by vision, and as a result, our ways of thinking are pervaded by visual metaphors. Consequently, the way we understand vision is bound to have important ramifications. Of particular interest for epistemology is the fact that numerous philosophers from Plato and Aristotle on have conceived of our intellect or understanding as analogous to the power of sight, so that knowing is regarded as like seeing.[10] Indeed, Descartes' notion of intuition places him within this tradition. This being the case, it is not accidental that epistemology and the theory of vision are closely intertwined; knowing is like seeing.

Because human beings rely so much on vision, it is rhetorically necessary for any philosopher whose metaphysics appears to clash with our visual experience to explain vision in a way that supports (or at least does not contradict) his or her metaphysics. Just as Berkeley developed a theory of vision to explain away the apparent contradiction between his immaterialism and the fact that we see objects as at a distance from us, so also Descartes wrote a theory of vision to reconcile his mechanistic metaphysics (that the only properties that really belong to things are geometric—size, shape, number, etc.—and motion) with the fact that we see objects as colored. Descartes is clearly aware of this need to reconcile his scientific picture of the world with our commonsense view of the world based on sense experience. Toward the end of the *Principles (Principia Philosophiae)*, he says:

> Up to now I have described this earth and indeed the whole visible universe as if it were a machine: I have considered only the various shapes and movements of its parts. But our senses show us much else besides—namely colours, smells, sounds and such-like; and if I were to say nothing about these it might be thought that I had left out the most important part of the explanation of the things in nature.[11]

To provide a complete account of nature, then, Descartes must develop a mechanistic theory of perception to explain our perception of the qualitative features of the world on the basis of the size, shape, motion, etc., of the parts of extended matter that make up physical objects. This is an especially challenging task for vision because mechanistic explanations of the sort Descartes is seeking to develop require action by contact, and objects do not touch our eyes—this is what makes vision somehow special and mysterious.

There are special reasons also for the importance of the theory of vision in the seventeenth century and for its significance in the struggle between the scholastics and the new mechanistic natural philosophy. For one thing, optics was extremely popular at this time. Most educated people were knowledgeable about the latest developments in optics, so that books on this subject would find an eager audience and thus be particularly influential. But more importantly, one of the key debates between Descartes and the scholastics was over "real qualities" and "substantial forms." Perception thus took on special significance in the debate, since Descartes believed that his opponents had assumed real qualities largely to explain sense perception. If this were so, then his ability to provide a successful mechanistic explanation of these phenomena would be a major victory—driving their theory from the field in the area where it was thought to be strongest. In the Sixth Replies Descartes says:

> Because the principal reason which moved philosophers to posit real accidents was that they thought that the perceptions of the senses could not be explained without assuming them, I have promised that I will explain these facts minutely with reference to each sense in my Physics. Not that I wish that any of my opinions should be taken on trust, but that I thought that those who have judged correctly in the matter of those accidents which I have already explained in the case of vision in my *Dioptrics* will easily guess what I am able to make good in the case of the others.[12]

The debate over the nature of color was particularly lively because at the time Descartes was writing, the study of light had been more or less relegated to the physicists, but colors were still regarded as the province of philosophers, and the resistance to a mechanistic explanation of colors was quite strong. Vasco Ronchi, a historian of theories of light, for example, hails Descartes' work on colors as an important part of the "battle to liberate colour from the clutches of the philosophers of the old school."[13]

A successful mechanistic explanation of vision would be a telling blow for Descartes against his scholastic opponents also since vision was traditionally regarded as the most spiritual of the senses because it can abstract forms from matter most perfectly (by contrast with, e.g., touch, which has the lowest power to do so). Because Descartes' mechanistic theory of vision essentially treats vision as a form of touch (the least spiritual of the senses, and one that is shared by all animals), it would be regarded as lowering humans to the level of the lower animals and thus would be particularly strongly opposed by the scholastics.[14]

Thus, Descartes' work on vision, far from being tangential to his main goals, is in fact very important to his plan of attack on the scholastics, and he sees it as such. It is, after all, in the *Dioptrics* and not in his more philosophical works that he claims to have finally laid to rest the theory of "intentional species" that played such a central role in scholastic epistemology.[15] And he apparently remained satisfied with his account of vision in the *Dioptrics* since he continues to refer his readers to it throughout his life without any indication that he envisioned any major revisions to it.[16]

I am focusing in this essay on the works in which Descartes develops his scientific account of vision in the most careful and systematic way. The most important text for this purpose is the *Dioptrics*, published in 1637 as an essay appended to the *Discourse on Method (Discours de la méthode pour bien conduire sa raison, et chercher la vérité dans les sciences)*. The *Meteorology (Les Météores)* also contains some significant remarks on color made in the course of his explanation of the rainbow. The posthumeously published works *The World (Le Monde: Traité de la Lumière)* and *Treatise on Man (Traité de L'Homme)* also include a great deal relevant to understanding Descartes' theory of vision—much of which is not included in the *Dioptrics*. The nature of light and the role of the animal spirits in perception, for example, receive much fuller treatment in the earlier unpublished works. I use material from these to supplement the account in the *Dioptrics* because the successful results Descartes reaches in the *Dioptrics, Meteorology,* etc., are, he says, based on his new method and on his physics, which he is withholding from publication.[17]

This focus on Descartes' scientific account of vision enables me to explain how philosophical issues arise for him in the context of a clearly defined task—namely, explaining how we visually perceive light, color, and the situation, distance, size, and shape of objects. I also connect his account of vision in these works with some of his subsequent remarks on vision. These are fragmentary and sometimes suggest modifications to his earlier views. This is especially true of the Sixth Replies, although Descartes himself glosses over the divergences from his earlier account. But his later remarks on vision where they differ from the earlier account can best be understood in light of Descartes' continuing attempt to wrestle with problems arising out of that earlier account.

Given that Descartes was, and saw himself as, engaged in a struggle against scholastic Aristotelianism, I develop my account of Descartes' theory of visual perception against the background of broadly Aristotelian doctrines about perception. While Descartes keeps many of the elements of the Aristotelian system, he rethinks it radically in order to harmonize it with his mind/body dualism and (relatedly) the need of the new physics for a mechanistic theory of nature. In showing exactly how and why Descartes is driven to diverge from the Aristotelian paradigm, I show how to attain a deeper and more accurate grasp of his thought about perception than one can reach by looking back at it through Locke, Berkeley, and Kant, as has so often been done by Anglo-American scholars.[18]

In presenting Descartes' thought against the background of scholastic Aristotelianism, I attempt as much as possible to be guided by the way Descartes perceives his opponents and the way he understands his own project in relation to them. His perception of scholastic philosophy was based, at least before 1640, on what he had studied at La Flèche. In 1640, anticipating objections to his *Meditations*, he wrote Marin Mersenne saying he had not read any scholastic philosophy in twenty years and asking him to recommend some authors.[19] In the letter he mentioned Toletus, Rubius (Ruvio), and the Coimbrans as authors he remembers from his student days, but these were only a few of the authors he would have studied, and we cannot be sure which of their books he read or how carefully he read them. Since he is so sparing of citations, scholars have resorted to seeking textual evidence of his indebtedness to this or that philosopher[20] and to researching the curriculum actually employed at La Flèche and other Jesuit colleges.[21] In general, Descartes would have been exposed to the basic Aristotelian corpus, together with commentaries and summaries of the opinions of various authorities on questions raised by the text. While Thomistic developments of Aristotle's thought would have been generally preferred by the Jesuits, they did not follow Thomas on all issues but often gave considerable weight to the opinions of intervening philosophers such as John Duns Scotus and William of Ockham and were, in general, known for a kind of "studied ecclecticism."[22] As one would expect, therefore, one thing that strikes Descartes about scholastic philosophy is the diversity of opinions among the scholars themselves.[23]

In spite of their diversity, however, Descartes perceives a kind of doctrinal unity among the scholastic philosophers. He wrote Mersenne in 1640 saying: "As for scholastic philosophy, I do not hold it as difficult to refute on account of the diversity of their opinions; for one can easily upset all the foundations about which they are in agreement among themselves; and that accomplished, all their particular disputes would appear inept."[24] How much doctrinal unity actually exists among the medieval and early modern scholastic Aristotelians is difficult to pin down. Certainly scholasticism was far from monolithic.[25] Yet it evolved out of a long tradition of commentaries on Aristotle's works, and its structure, vocabulary, and content were deeply shaped by this, so that such diverse thinkers as Thomas Aquinas, Scotus, Ockham, and the textbook writers of the late sixteenth and early seventeenth centuries could all consider themselves to be Aristotelians. What is important for our purposes, however, is that Descartes himself perceives the philosophy of the schools to be based on common foundations, and he takes those foundations to be Aristotelian in character. This perception is, I believe, strengthened by two factors—one institutional and external, and the other a function of his own habits of mind.

On an institutional level, the Jesuits (who, in the wake of the Reformation, were very wary of any innovations) stressed very heavily the authority of Thomas Aquinas and Aristotle. Following their founder, St. Ignatius, the Jesuits adhered strictly to the doctrines of St. Thomas in theology. Outside the realm of theology, however, they followed Aristotle. The *Ratio Studiorum* of 1583 issued by the General of the Society of Jesus made this explicit, stating that "in logic, natural philosophy, ethics and metaphysics, Aristotle's doctrine is to be followed."[26] This gave Aristotle primacy as an authority in the area Descartes was most interested in—namely, natural philosophy. The very real threat of sanctions against those who opposed Aristotle[27] no doubt contributed to the appearance of doctrinal unity and led philosophers to try to cite Aristotle in support of their views wherever possible and to downplay their differences from him.[28]

In understanding how Descartes perceives the scholastics, we must also consider the way Descartes' own foundationalist approach to philosophy influences his perception of them. He quite naturally believes that if scholastic philosophy has reached a dead end and can yield no useful results,[29] the reason is that it is based on the wrong foundations—and it was Aristotle, after all, who set out the principles upon which scholastic philosophy was built. He thus thinks in terms of replacing Aristotle's principles with his own. As he said to Mersenne in 1641:

> I may tell you between ourselves, that these six *Meditations* contain the entire foundations for my physics. But it is not necessary to say so, if you please, since that might make it harder for those who favor Aristotle to approve them. I hope that those who read them will gradually accustom themselves to my principles and recognize the truth in them before they notice that they destroy those of Aristotle.[30]

His own strategy for dealing with the scholastics, then, is not to refute them directly but rather to sweep aside the whole scholastic tradition and begin to build anew on foundations of his own. As he said to Mersenne in 1641: "I have completely lost the intent to refute this philosophy; for I see that it is so absolutely and so clearly destroyed by means of the establishment of my philosophy alone, that no other refutation is needed."[31] Since laying new foundations for science was his main ambition, it was not, therefore, essential to his goal to distinguish carefully between Aristotle's views and later accretions to them or distortions of them.[32] He may well deliberately make use of some of the more implausible "scholastic" opinions for rhetorical effect—as, for example, when he mocks the "little intentional species which fly through the air."[33]

In light of Descartes' perception of scholastic philosophy as based on the principles of Aristotle, I provide the relevant texts from Aristotle as background for my discussion of Descartes and draw out the most basic features of the conceptual framework within which Aristotle explains perception. For the most part, I focus on features of Aristotle's thought so general and so widely shared by Aristotelians of all stripes that detailed consideration of intermediary sources is unnecessary. I do, however, bring in Thomistic developments of Aristotle where these are relevant to my argument, since Descartes' understanding of Aristotle was influenced by commentators who were broadly (although not exclusively) within the Thomistic tradition. And I also indicate briefly what some of the main controversies among seventeenth-century Aristotelians were, since this is helpful in understanding why Descartes felt it necessary to break so radically with the whole tradition. Furthermore, in some cases Aristotle has no explanation to offer at all (for example, in the perception of situation and distance), and in others Aristotle's views were known by Descartes to be wholly erroneous (as, for example, his understanding of the structure and function of the eye). In these cases I briefly summarize Descartes' more immediate predecessors in the perspectivist tradition.

I begin by examining Descartes' account of perception in Rule XII, for it is here that he first presents a systematic account of perception, confronting the traditional one rooted in the *De Anima*. This account, however, is for Descartes merely a kind of outline or program that must be fleshed out with the details of the perceptual process.

In chapter 2, I examine the foundation for Descartes' projected mechanization of visual perception—his purely mechanistic account of the objects of vision, light, and color.

In chapter 3, I examine Descartes' mechanization of the processes occurring within the perceiver—the formation of the retinal image, its transmission via the nerves into the cerebral cavities, and the elaborate mechanisms involving the animal spirits and the pineal gland. Because he has very little information about the actual structure and function of the visual system, Descartes' speculations about these are shaped by his philosophical presuppositions, among which is the belief that to explain our perception of a unified object, it is necessary that a unified image be present on a physiological level (and hence the supposition that the two retinal images must be merged at the pineal gland).

The mechanisms described in chapter 3 would appear to explain successfully our perception of light and color. The problem is, however, that while they would explain how we perceive a two-dimensional mosaic of light and color (which is a duplicate of the retinal image), we do not, in fact, perceive things as they are represented in the retinal image. Thus the mechanisms already described must be supplemented to explain situation, distance, size, and shape perception. At this point, Descartes introduces a kind of inner homunculus who corrects for the defects in the retinal image. Descartes' unsuccessful attempt to integrate the mechanical model and the homunculus model in his explanation of visual spatial perception is the subject of chapter 4.

1

Descartes' Thought about Perception in Rule XII

THE *RULES (REGULAE AD DIRECTIONEM INGENII)*, NEVER PUBLISHED DURING Descartes' lifetime but believed to have been completed around 1628, provides a valuable starting point for understanding Descartes' theory of vision. The account of perception in Rule XII illustrates both his continuity with and his fundamental break from the Aristotelian framework for explaining perception and provides a preview of the basic type of program that he intends to follow in his own explanation.

Rule XII contains Descartes' first systematic discussion of perception. Some features of his discussion appear similar to the stock Aristotelian/Thomistic account commonly taught in the schools. Explanations of this fact, however, vary. Some hold that he had not yet broken free of the scholastic way of thinking and that the *Rules* thus represents a transitional phase in his thinking that was superseded by his later writings. Others hold that the *Rules* articulates already deep and enduring features of Descartes' thought that are radically different from Aristotle, so that the *Rules* is central to any understanding of his later works.

Among those who regard the *Rules* as an important key to Descartes' thought is Jean-Luc Marion. In *Sur l'ontologie grise de Descartes* he argues that Descartes in the *Rules* is deliberately and self-consciously taking a position vis-à-vis the basic Aristotelian corpus that he had been taught in school, and Marion carefully documents all the connections with and divergences from the relevant Aristotelian texts. He calls the *Rules* both a denial of the Aristotelian ontology and a transposed resumption ("reprise transposée") of its themes.[1] According to Marion, Descartes is using Aristotelian terminology while attempting subtly to shift the meanings of the terms—bending them to accomodate his own thought. Marion therefore adopts a heuristic device of generating a sort of dialogue between Aristotle and Descartes, and he sets Descartes' texts opposite the corresponding Aristotelian texts in order to illustrate connections between the two and pinpoint the ways in which Descartes diverges from Aristotle. In doing so he ignores intermediate thinkers, and he cites in support of this the passage in Rule IV where Descartes states his intention of avoiding the way terms have been recently used in the schools.[2] There are, Marion argues, "des filations historiques plus nombreuses, à la limite, entre Descartes et Aristote, qu'entre lui et les neoscholastiques (les *Regulae* ignorent quasi tout les opinions specifiques aux recentoires, et recusent même explicitement les auteurs des 'derniers temps')."[3]

Without passing judgment on the truth of Marion's thesis for the *Rules* as a whole, the account of perception in Rule XII, at least, is clearly a reworking of Aristotle's account in the *De Anima*, a text that was certainly familiar to Descartes—together, of course, with those commentaries on it commonly used in the Jesuit colleges during this period, such as those of the Coimbrans *De Anima* author Emmanuel de Goes, Toletus, and Ruvio. Since these commentators were coming predominantly (although not exclusively) out of the Thomistic tradition, I follow Aquinas' interpretation of Aristotle on most disputed points. I also indicate briefly what some of the main controversies were at the time Descartes was writing, since his attempt in the *Rules* to sketch out a radically new way to explain perception bypassing all the scholastic concepts was in part a response to what he took to be the confusions and insuperable problems inherent in their views. Understanding these disputes is therefore of help in seeing why Descartes made the changes he did.

The Traditional Aristotelian Account

Like Descartes' account in the *Rules*, Aristotle's account of perception in the *De Anima* remains at an abstract level and does not bring in physics or physiology. It articulates the basic conceptual framework into which more concrete data is to be integrated. Of central importance for understanding that framework are Aristotle's understanding of the soul and the distinctions between act and potency, matter and form, and proper and common sensibles. Following a brief sketch of these concepts, I will examine in more detail how the Aristotelians employ them in explaining the function of the external senses, the internal senses, and the intellect.

CONCEPTUAL FRAMEWORK

The soul is the act or form of the body as a whole ("the first grade of actuality of a natural body having life potentially in it"[4]) and is that from which all its powers originate. It is qua informed by an animal soul that the animal senses or moves and qua informed by a rational soul that the person thinks, but it is the composite that senses or thinks. There is no suggestion in the *De Anima*, however, that the soul is located exclusively in any body part.[5] Acceptance of this definition of the soul is one of the distinguishing marks of the Aristotelian tradition (by contrast with Platonists or Augustinians). St. Thomas and his followers espoused it, and it is quoted virtually verbatim in the standard textbooks of Descartes' time.[6]

There was some controversy over whether Aristotle should be interpreted as saying that human beings possess three souls (nutritive, sensitive, and rational) or only one, but the view that we possess only one (with the rational soul bringing with it the powers of the two lower souls, which were then called "faculties" of the soul) was defended by Aquinas. By the time of the Council of Trent (1545–63), it was the one generally accepted by the Church. Certainly this is how Descartes would have been taught Aristotle. Considerable dispute still existed about how to describe the relationship between the human (rational) soul and its organic faculties (nutritive and sensitive). Are the faculties to be understood as really distinct from the soul, or were they merely modalities of its operation?[7] Are the organic faculties present in the soul as in a subject, or in the body?[8] Is the rational soul present from conception?[9] In spite of the controversies about the relationship between the rational soul and its sensitive and nutritive faculties, however, the Aristotelians were still united in their belief that the soul is the form of the body and not a distinct substance, and they regarded sensation as one of the powers of the soul, albeit one that the soul necessarily exercises in and through corporeal organs.

Another fundamental feature of Aristotle's thought is his empiricism. In spite of his belief in the immateriality of the intellect (or "nous"), he holds that all knowledge has its source in sensation, and sensation is understood as a process in which the perceiver is purely receptive. For vision, this implies a rejection of any sort of emission theory, such as those of Plato or Galen. Our senses must be understood as in potency relative to their objects and can sense only when acted on by those objects, just as the combustible requires the presence of something from outside to make it burn. Otherwise we could sense things at will, which we cannot do. Sensation occurs, in the one who senses, but whenever sensation occurs, we have the sense object acting in the organism. Furthermore, the very act by which the sense faculty that is potentially, say, colored becomes actually informed with the form of a particular color *is* the act of the sense object that is bringing this about (*DA*, 426a2–20). Potency in the Aristotelian sense, then, is not mere passivity, in that the sense faculty is brought to the act of sensing by the reception of the form of the object.[10] Each sense is in potency relative to its own objects only: sight to color, hearing to sound, etc.

Flowing from this, then, is the important distinction between proper and common sensibles—proper sensibles being those sense objects perceivable by one sense only (e.g., color or sound) and the common sensibles being those perceivable by more than one sense (e.g., shape or motion). This distinction is very important to Aristotle's account of perception and distinguishes him from atomists like Democritus who explain our perception of savors, for example, on the basis of the size and shape of the atoms. For Aristotle the qualitative is as real as the quantitative, and this is a constant feature of Aristotelian physics.

Descartes' reduction of the proper sensibles to the common sensibles, which is apparent already in the *Rules*, was one thing that particularly evoked the ire of the Aristotelians and led them to see him as reviving ancient atomism.[11]

Finally, the distinction between matter and form is essential to Aristotle's account. He says, "By a 'sense' is meant what has the power of receiving into itself the sensible forms of things without the matter" (424a16–17). Aristotle says very little about how forms exist in the sense faculty or in the medium for that matter, and his successors tried to fill in this gap. St. Thomas follows Aristotle in taking sensation to involve the reception of the sensible forms of things (by contrast with their substantial forms) without their matter but often uses the term *species* in place of form when speaking of form as it exists in the perceiver. The understanding of what species are, both in the medium and in the perceiver, was one of the most extensively debated issues in the period between Aquinas and Descartes. Indeed, the issues became so staggeringly complex and the proliferation of different types of *species* got so out of hand that many philosophers, following Ockham (who identified himself as an Aristotelian), decided to eliminate the notion altogether, going so far as to accept action at a distance in order to do so. Many philosophers, however, were unwilling to accept action at a distance, and the term *species* was still very widely used, especially in Thomist circles and in many textbooks.[12]

Having now completed my summary of the basic conceptual framework employed by the Aristotelians, I turn to the way they explained the operation of the external senses, the internal senses (common sense, imagination, and memory), and the intellect in perception in order to provide a basis of comparison for Descartes' discussion of each of these in Rule XII.

External Senses

All animals possess the faculty of sensation (one of the powers of the sensitive soul), and this operates through the sense organs. Sensation is a reception of forms without matter (*DA*, 424a16–17). Unlike plants, animals have sense organs that can receive the forms of objects without their matter. This is possible both because of the physical constitution of the sense organ and the fact that it is part of a living being with a sensitive soul; the soul can exercise its faculties only in appropriately organized matter. The sense faculty resides in the material organ, but it is not identical with it: "What perceives is, of course, a spatial magnitude, but we must not admit that either the having the power to perceive or the sense itself is a magnitude; what they are is a certain ratio or power in a magnitude" (*DA*, 424a25–28).

In the case of senses that involve an external medium, the material organ must be composed primarily of the element that serves as a medium for that quality and must be in some sense neutral with regard to the extremes of the qualities it discerns. This can take the form of a complete absence of the quality it discerns (as the water in the eye is colorless), or it can take the form of having the quality but being in the middle range between extremes. Thus the flesh cannot be too hot or too cold, too hard or too soft. What occurs in sensation is that: "What has the power of sensation is potentially like what the perceived object is actually; that is, while at the beginning of the process of its being acted upon the two interacting factors are dissimilar, at the end the one acted upon is assimilated to the other and is identical in quality with it" (*DA*, 418a3–6). Although a physical change occurs in the sense organ when it takes on the form of the sense object, sensation is not to be understood as identical with that change. The hand may become warm when feeling a warm object, but it does not become hard or rough when feeling a hard or rough object. There is a kind of rudimentary abstraction of form from matter even in this first stage of perception.[13]

Aquinas follows Aristotle here, saying "external sense cognition is brought about solely by the immutation of the sense by the sensible. Hence by the form which is impressed by the sensible, sensation takes place."[14] Elaborating on the nature of the immutation, he makes explicit what was implicit in Aristotle—namely, that the sort of immutation that occurs in sensation is not merely a physical change. He distinguishes natural immutation (where the form is received according to its natural existence, as when heat is received from a hot body) and spiritual immutation (where the form is received according to a spiritual mode of existence, as when the form of color is received into the pupil of the eye without making it colored). In sensation a spiritual immutation is required, whereby "an intention of the sensible form is effected in the sense organ."[15]

The centuries separating Aquinas and Descartes were especially fertile in work on perception,[16] and rival traditions sprang up which differed slightly in their terminology and approach to the material. During this period, Thomists devoted considerable work to clarifying what was meant by a "spiritual immutation," what "intentional existence" was, and how physical objects could possibly produce a "spiritual immutation" in the senses.[17] The terminology of *impressed species* and *expressed species* was widely used in Thomist circles. The external sense organ received an impressed species through the action of the sensible object upon it, but different opinions were held on whether or not the external sense produces an expressed species (or image).[18] The complexities generated by those who tried to clarify intentional existence and to explain what impressed and expressed species were led a growing number of philosophers to be very dissatisfied with "species" and to wish to eliminate them altogether although no very satisfactory substitute had been found.[19] Descartes, having been educated by the Jesuits, would have been exposed to the Thomistic tradition but was probably familiar with many other writers who employed the term in various ways. His intention (already apparent in the *Rules*) to provide a mechanistic substitute for the traditional notion of species, however, was not out of place in the intellectual milieu of the seventeenth century, given the widespread discontent with the notion of "species" and growing interest in mechanistic explanations.

INTERNAL SENSES

The process of perception is not, however, complete in the sense organ alone; it is necessary to account for how the input from the five senses is integrated—and for this Aristotle postulates what he calls the common sense. In the *De Anima* he argues that we must postulate a unified sense faculty in order to explain our ability to discriminate between, for example, white and sweet (426b12 to 427a14). The other functions of the common sense are many, including perception of the common sensibles, correcting the deliverances of one sense by those of another, and reflexive self-awareness. It is not, however, a sixth sense in addition to the proper senses, but rather a power that the senses possess when acting together. Or as Ross puts it: "We must think of sense as a single faculty which for certain purposes is specified into the five senses, but discharges certain functions in virtue of its generic nature."[20]

Conceptually, several further stages must be distinguished in order to account for our sensory knowledge. First, the impressions or movements arising from sensation must be continued beyond just the organs themselves, which is the function of the imagination. The imagination is, Aristotle says, "that in virtue of which an image (phantasm) arises for us" (428a1–2). The sensitive imagination is common to all animals and plays a very important role in explaining the movements of animals, since their actions are determined by how objects appear to them. Humans also possess deliberative imagination in virtue of which we are able to form phantasms at will by joining together phantasms of the perceptual type, and this is particularly important for practical reasons. Imagination is also important for conceptual thought. Aristotle says, "But to the thinking soul images serve as if they were contents of perception," and "the soul never thinks without an image" (*DA*, 431a14–16).[21]

The common sense and the imagination, as faculties of the sensitive soul, are dependent upon the intactness and unity of the sensitive body for their ability to exercise their functions, but Aristotle refrains from simply identifying either of them with a specific physical organ. There are some indications in his physiological writings that he took the heart to be the seat of the common sense.[22] But even if one did concede that the heart is the *seat* of the common sense, as some commentators suggest, it would still not be identical with the heart considered as a physical organ, but would be a power or actuality of the heart (see *DA*, 424a25–28). The same is true of the faculty of imagination that, while having a physical basis in the movements conveyed inward from the senses, is nonetheless not merely reduced to some spatially localized body part.

The last of the faculties mentioned by Aristotle is memory, which retains the phantasms of the imagination in such a way that they can be recalled. Aristotle says very little about memory in the *De Anima*. But in *De Memoria*, he says that it has its seat in some part of the body and notes that perceptions leave traces there, much like the impressions made by a seal.[23]

Aristotle's understanding of the internal senses (a title given them by his successors) underwent considerable development during the medieval period, although their basic function remained the same. The internal senses were understoood as integrating the input from the five external senses and producing a phantasm or image. Various commentators treated them differently and disagreed about how many internal senses there are.[24] Some efforts were made to identify the organs or ventricles of the brain that served as the seat of imagination or of memory, but, like Aristotle, his successors saw this as a matter of discovering through which organs the soul exercises various powers, rather than identifying the faculty with that organ (as Descartes was to do).

Aquinas settled on four internal senses: common sense, imagination, memory (which he treats very much as Aristotle does), and a fourth that he calls the estimative/cogitative sense. The estimative sense in animals serves for the "apprehension of intentions which are not received through the senses" (as for example the harmfulness of the wolf is perceived by the sheep) and is the highest sense possessed by animals. In humans it is called the cogitative sense or discursive power because a kind of interplay occurs between reason and sense in humans enabling them to perceive the advantages and dangers of things in a way that goes beyond instinct.[25] Later Thomists kept the same four senses as Aquinas, but refined and developed his theory.

In the sixteenth century, however, there was a significant trend toward streamlining the account of the internal senses and eliminating the estimative or cogitative sense. By 1600 most writers either conflated all the internal senses into one, usually called imagination, or else returned to those explicitly mentioned by Aristotle.[26] Descartes follows this latter tradition and refers in the *Rules* only to the senses Aristotle mentions, although he does say that animal motion is a result of movements in the corporeal imagination, which thus must do the work of the Thomistic estimative sense.

Intellect

Aristotle in the *De Anima* is extraordinarily cryptic in his description of the intellect and the way in which it connects with the senses. He says, "And in fact mind as we have described it is what it is by virtue of becoming all things, while there is another which is what it is by virtue of making all things: this is a sort of positive state like light; for in a sense light makes potential colors into actual colors. Mind in this sense of it is separable, impassible, unmixed, since it is in its essential nature activity" (430a14–19). The brevity and obscurity of Aristotle's deliverances on the subject of what came to be called the active (or agent) intellect and the passive (or potential) intellect and the importance of the topic— particularly for those who wished to defend the immortality of the soul—led to considerable controversy about this topic.

Aquinas interpreted Aristotle as saying that there is within each individual a passive or potential intellect (which knows by receiving intelligible species) and an active intellect, which is ultimately a special power given each individual by God. The active intellect performs the task of abstracting the intelligible species from the phantasms presented by the internal senses and impressing them on the passive intellect.[27]

During the period between Aquinas and Descartes, controversies raged about the intellect. These included the debate over whether the active intellect was a part of each soul or whether there was only one for all (the problem of the "unicity of the intellect"); the question of whether the active and passive intellects are really distinct;[28] the question of whether immediate intellection of singulars was possible;[29] the way in which the intelligible species is produced; and the question of whether the immortality of the soul can be proved by natural reason.[30] In spite of these controversies, however, most authors took the agent intellect to be necessary to explain how the intelligible species are abstracted from the phantasms supplied by the imagination.[31] Descartes, as will be shown, takes the intellect or understanding to be a unitary power and makes no reference to anything like the Aristotelian/Thomistic active intellect in his account of sense perception—a fact that was to have important implications since the active intellect had played such a key role in the process of abstraction that was central to the traditional epistemology.

Descartes' Account in Rule XII

Descartes in Rule XII attempts a radical simplification of the scholastic theory of perception. He declines to give a complete account what the mind and body are, or of how the body is informed by the soul, since he wishes to "make no assertions on matters which are apt to give rise to controversy, without first setting out the reasons which led me to make them."[32] But it is clear his radical mind/body dualism is already present and operative. As I show in what follows, he has eliminated virtually the whole traditional Aristotelian conceptual apparatus, and the traces of faculty psychology that linger in his discussion of the common sense, imagination, and memory are merely vestigial.

Before beginning his account of perception he remarks:

> Of course you are not obliged to believe that things are as I suggest. But what is to prevent you from following these suppositions if it is obvious that they detract not a jot from the truth of things, but simply make everything much clearer? This is just what you do in geometry when you make certain assumptions about quantity, which in no way weaken the force of the demonstrations, even though in physics you often take a different view of the nature of quantity.[33]

Indeed, one thing that is striking about his brief discussion of perception in Rule XII is the frequent occurrence of disclaimers of this sort. These indicate that in spite of the superficial similarity between his view and those of the scholastics, Descartes anticipated opposition from them, which he was attempting to head off (and thus he must at some point have envisioned publishing the *Rules*). In addition, he is already trying to move the reader in the direction of thinking in a purely quantitative way as opposed to the way the Aristotelians thought about physics, and he continues to do this throughout his discussion of perception.

I turn now to the details of his account, in order to show precisely how and where Descartes has broken with the traditional view.

THE EXTERNAL SENSES

The Aristotelians, as previously discussed, characterize sensation as the reception of forms without matter. Each external sense is in potency relative to its own proper object, and when stimulated by its proper object, it passes from potency to act in such a way that it becomes informed with the form of the object. Descartes' account bears a superficial resemblance to their theory. He even uses Aristotle's example—the comparison to the reception of a seal by a piece of wax. However, there are several key differences.

First, Descartes does not regard the senses as in potency to their objects as do the Aristotelians, but as merely passive: "Insofar as our external senses are all parts of the body, sense perception, strictly speaking, is merely passive [*passionem*]. . . . sense perception occurs in the same way in which wax takes on an impression [*figuram*] from a seal."[34]

Within the scholastic tradition, each sense is in potency only to its own proper object—sight to colors, the tongue to savors, etc. Passivity has no such connotations and signifies only the general state of being acted upon. According to the traditional view, when the sense is acted upon, it goes from potency to act, the act of the sense faculty and that of the sense object being postulated to be one and the same. Seeing the external sense as only passive does not allow for this sort of act. What occurs in the sense organ has been materialized by Descartes, as becomes clear in his treatment of the wax analogy, and thus can be only local motion.

The second major Aristotelian concept to be discarded is that of "form," and Descartes replaces it with figure or shape. This is clear in Descartes' use of the wax-seal example. Aristotle uses the wax and seal example as an analogy only; Descartes intends us to take it more literally. In *De Anima*, Aristotle says:

> By a "sense" is meant what has the power of receiving into itself the sensible forms of things without the matter. This must be conceived of as taking place in the way in which a piece of wax takes on the impress of a signet ring without the iron or gold; we say that what produces the impression is a signet of bronze or gold, but its particular metallic constitution makes no difference: in a similar way the sense is affected by what is colored or flavored or sounding, but it is indifferent what in each case the *substance* is; what alone matters is what *quality* it has. (424a17–24)

Thus, when Aristotle speaks of the sense receiving into itself the sensible forms, he does not mean sensible shapes. The quality affecting the sense might be, for example, color, heat, or sweetness. Thus, the sense receives the form without the matter in a way merely analogous to the way the wax receives the shape of the ring. The "form" received by the sense is itself something immaterial, although it is not received in a purely immaterial way by the senses as it will be by the intellect. A physical change does occur in the sense organ, but it is not the sort of literal taking of an imprint suggested by the wax-seal analogy.

Descartes, however, states:

> Sense perception occurs in the same way in which wax takes on an impression from a seal. It should not be thought that I have a mere analogy in mind here: we must think of the external shape of the sentient body as being really changed by the object in exactly the same way as the shape of the surface of the wax is altered by the seal. This is the case, we must admit, not only when we feel some body as having a shape, as being hard or rough to the touch etc., but also when we have a tactile perception of heat or cold and the like. The same is true of the other senses: thus, in the eye, the first opaque membrane receives the shape impressed upon it by multi-colored light; and in the ears, the nose and the tongue, the first membrane which is impervious to the passage of the object thus takes on a new shape from the sound, the smell and the flavor respectively. [35]

The sense organs are directly acted upon mechanically by their objects (there can be no action at a distance for Descartes), and this results in certain changes in the figure or motion of the membranes of the sense organ. There is no essential difference from what happens to a piece of wax except that the membranes in the sense organs are more fine and delicate so that they can be easily moved by the fine particles involved in the transmission of, say, light. What is received is no longer an immaterial form but merely a physical alteration of figure or motion. There is no "spiritual immutation" or reference to the "intentional existence" of the sensible form in the sense organ of the sort Aquinas and subsequent Thomists postulated.

A third major difference between Descartes' account and that of his scholastic opponents, which is apparent in Rule XII, is that he is moving clearly in the direction of denying the distinction between proper and common sensibles that is so essential to the Aristotelians, and he intends to treat figure and motion as the objects of all the senses alike.

He is cautious about denying the existence of proper sensibles, but it is clearly implied by what he says. It is hard to see how light and color could move the membrane in the eye in just the same way as the seal does the wax unless they are material in nature and possessed of some figure. This reading is corroborated by the way he speaks of the membranes in the organs being "impervious to the passage of the object and in this way having their figure altered." Thus what acts upon all the sense organs alike is only particles in motion—a view that is more like that of Democritus than Aristotle.

That this is, in fact, the direction Descartes' thought is taking here is corroborated by the fact that he again launches into an attempt to persuade the reader that the assumptions he is making are really quite harmless and do not deny accepted ideas about color, but are merely useful hypotheses. He says:

> This is a most helpful way of conceiving these matters, since nothing is more readily perceivable by the senses than shape, for it can be touched as well as seen. Moreover, the consequences of this supposition are no more false than those of any other. This is demonstrated by the fact that the concept of shape is so simple and common that it is involved in everything perceivable by the senses. Take color, for example: whatever you may suppose color to be, you will not deny that it is extended and consequently has shape. So what troublesome consequences could there be if—while avoiding the useless assumption and pointless invention of some new entity, and without denying what others have preferred to think on the subject—we simply make an abstraction, setting aside every feature of color apart from its possessing the character of shape, and conceive of the difference between white, blue, red, etc. as being like the difference between the following figures or similar ones?[36] (See fig. 1.1.)

But simply because colored things also possess shape, this surely does not show that color possesses the character of shape, or as Haldane and Ross translate the phrase, "possesses the nature of figure." It might be that Descartes is merely saying that the difference between colors, or other sensory qualities, is only analogous to the difference between various figures, but this seems less likely when we look at the concluding sentences of this paragraph (which end his discussion of the external senses): "The same can be said about everything

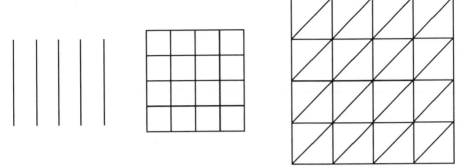

Figure 1.1

perceivable by the senses, since it is certain that the infinite multiplicity of figures is sufficient for the expression [*exprimendis*] of all the differences in perceptible things."

The term translated "expression" here is rather vague and open ended. La Fleur translates it "explain,"[37] and indeed in his later works, it is to figure and motion that Descartes turns to explain the operation of all our senses. The fact that Descartes does not mention motion here may or may not be significant. Certainly motion later plays an important role in his explanation of color. Apparently Descartes, still working with the more static wax and seal model, has not yet come to the more thoroughgoing and sophisticated mechanism of *The World, Treatise on Man,* and *Dioptrics.*

Even the claim that all differences in sensible objects can be expressed by different figures would be questioned by an Aristotelian. Since tastes and colors are qualitatively different sorts of things, it would be hard to see how the difference between, say, sour and blue could conceivably be expressed as a difference between figures. Thus, although he has held back from saying explicitly that there are no "real qualities" or proper sensibles out there or that figure and motion are the objects of all the senses alike, that is clearly the direction he is moving in, and the distinction between proper and common sensibles has essentially been discarded.

INTERNAL SENSES: COMMON SENSE, IMAGINATION, AND MEMORY

For Descartes, as for the Aristotelians, more is involved in perception than the external senses alone; the common sense and the imagination are also necessary. The changes Descartes has made in the Aristotelian understanding of the external senses necessitate equally radical changes in his understanding of the internal senses. The elimination of forms or species from his account of the external senses, of course, means that he cannot rely on them in discussing the internal senses. Both the nature and the function of the internal senses change; they are materialized and identified with specific body parts, and their function is reduced to merely transmitting patterns of figures and motions.

Descartes' discussion of the common sense is quite sketchy. He says:

> When an external sense organ is stimulated by an object, the figure which it receives is conveyed at one and the same moment to another part of the body known as the "common sense," without any entity really passing from the one to the other. In exactly the same way I understand that while I am writing, at the very moment when individual letters are traced on the paper, not only does the point of the pen move, but the slightest motion of this part cannot but be transmitted simultaneously to the whole pen. All these various motions are traced out in the air by the tip of the quill, even though I do not conceive of anything real passing from one end to the other.[38]

Whether the common sense is to be identified with the tip of the pen or with what it writes on is not entirely clear, but it is clear that he has broken with the Aristotelian tradition by simply materializing the common sense and identifying it with a part of the body. Its function has also changed in that it does not perform the sorts of integrative functions it performs for Aristotle (integrating input from several senses, checking the reports of one sense against those of another, etc.). It receives a pattern of figure and motion and impresses that same pattern on the imagination.[39] No mention is made of forms or species but merely of changes in the figure and motion of body parts.

The imagination and memory are similarly treated:

> The common sense functions like a seal, fashioning in the phantasy, as if in wax, the same figures or ideas [figuras vel ideas] which come, pure and without body, from the external senses. The phantasy is a genuine part of the body, and is large enough to allow different parts of it to take on many different figures and, generally, to retain them for some time; in which case it is to be identified with what we call memory.[40]

This passage emphasizes very strongly the purely corporeal character of the imagination and memory. The comparison with wax, the references to the imagination being big enough so that the figures can be kept distinct from each other, and the parts retaining impressions also lead the reader to think of the figures received by the imagination in a very literal way—as impressions in some soft substance.

There are, however, several statements in this passage that do not seem to fit this sort of mechanistic, materialistic interpretation. Descartes speaks of "figures and ideas"—a surprisingly incongruous conjunction. And he says that they come "pure and without body from the external senses" (a sensibus externis puras et sine corpore venientes) or, according to Haldane and Ross, "uncontaminated and without any bodily admixture."[41] How are we to interpret these phrases? Is Descartes trying to elevate figure to be some sort of quasi-spiritual intermediary between mind and matter, since he speaks of the figures or ideas coming "pure and without body" from the senses?[42] I believe we should be very cautious about attributing such a theory to Descartes here; on the contrary, there is nothing in these passages that cannot be reconciled with a completely materialistic mechanism. The phrase "pure and without any bodily admixture," for example, can be interpreted in the same way as the phrase "without the passage of any real entity." In other words, it is not the figure transmitted that is "pure and without bodily admixture" (and thus somehow partially spiritual), rather it is that the mode of transmission does not involve the transmission of some material thing, such as little copies or eidola. If the upper end of the pen traces figures in a piece of wax, those figures are not somehow spiritual just because nothing material has passed from one end of the pen to the other. On the contrary, Descartes emphasizes the fact that these figures take up some space in the imagination.

His puzzling conjunction of "figures or ideas," however, is difficult to explain. Does he mean to treat the two as synonyms? If so, how could ideas be impressed in a purely corporeal imagination as he describes? The phrase in question can doubtless be read as an attempt, perhaps unconscious, to upgrade "figure" so that the transition to the understanding will be smoother. It could be read equally well, however, as materializing ideas. After all, in *Treatise on Man,* Descartes says that the figures traced in the surface of the pineal gland by the departing animal spirits "must be taken for ideas, that is to say, for the forms or images which the reasonable soul considers immediately when, united to this machine, she imagines or senses some object."[43]

Descartes' account of the internal senses in Rule XII is, then, simply an extension of his mechanistic explanation of what occurs in the external sense organ. Since he has rejected the key element in the Aristotelian theory—namely, forms (or species)—he develops instead a theory in which the *figure* impressed on the external sense is transmitted mechanically to the imagination.[44]

I turn now to the last stage in the perceptual process—the interaction between the imagination and the understanding.

THE UNDERSTANDING

Given the changes Descartes has already made in the Aristotelian account, major changes become necessary in his account of the interaction between the imagination and the understanding. He says, "The power through which we know things in the strict sense is purely spiritual, and is no less distinct from the whole body than blood is distinct from bone, or the hand from the eye."[45] It is at this point that Descartes' problems become acute. As discussed in the preceding sections, he has thrown out the Aristotelian metaphysical distinctions between act and potency and between matter and form. He has not brought in any of the somewhat more complicated machinery elaborated by the Thomistic tradition on the basis of the Aristotelian texts: impressed species, expressed species, phantasms, the agent intellect, the possible intellect, etc. Although he condemns the scholastics, he fails to offer his own theory of abstraction to fill the gap, and this is a serious deficiency of his account.[46] Put simply, the problem is that he has figure (and perhaps motion) conveyed to the imagination, but the mechanical wax-seal model cannot be extended to the link with the understanding, since this latter is purely incorporeal. Descartes himself states that the cognitive power "is sometimes passive sometimes active; sometimes resembling the seal, sometimes the wax. But this should be understood merely as an analogy, for nothing quite like this power is to be found in corporeal things."[47]

This account of the understanding contains some parallels with the traditional account—for example, the immateriality of the intellect and the view that it is both active and passive in perception. But while the Aristotelian tradition had supposed both an active and a passive intellect, Descartes does not. One and the same understanding is sometimes active and sometimes passive in relation to the imagination. And given Descartes' radical mind/body dualism and his elimination of the Aristotelian notions of actuality and potentiality, the interaction between imagination and the understanding must take on a very different character from the one it has for the Aristotelians.

Given the degree to which Descartes' thought is pervaded by mechanism, he cannot but think of the mind as acting upon the body in terms of the mind producing changes in the figures and motions of various parts of the brain. Although he cannot conceive of the action of the body upon the mind in this way, he treats the whole process up to the last step wholly mechanistically. He speaks in the *Dioptrics* of "the movements of which the picture [pineal gland image] is composed acting immediately on [*agissant contre*] our mind"—clearly conceiving of the motions as pressing on or bumping up against the soul.[48] All this differs vastly from the subtle (albeit mysterious) interplay of phantasms, active intellect, and passive intellect, which gives birth to intelligibility and results in a union between knower and known in Aristotle.[49]

The understanding, Descartes says, "can be stimulated by the imagination, or act upon it." The mind is described as seeing and touching when it "applies itself along with the imagination to the common sense" or as imagining or conceiving when "applying itself to the imagination in order to form new figures." And if it acts on its own, it is said to "understand." But it is really the incorporeal mind that in all these cases enables us to know.[50] The mind or understanding, then, perceives in cooperation with the internal senses, but how this sort of cooperation can occur is not explained. He simply states that it does.

Descartes does not seem aware in these passages of the seriousness of the problem he faces in explaining the interaction of the understanding and the imagination. And one reason for this, I suggest, is the shifting terminology that he uses to describe what is transmitted. In discussing the link between the understanding and the imagination, he uses the terms *impression, idea, figure,* and *image* interchangeably. His thought at this point is obviously in a rather inchoate state. Figures or impressions as he understands them are wholly corporeal, but he wants them to do the same job that the forms or species of the tradition did, so he tries to blur their corporeal nature by throwing in terms like *idea* and *image*. *Idea* has more of a mental connotation, and *image* seems to hover between the two. Although such shifting and ambiguous use of terminology cannot really solve Descartes' problem, it does paper over the gap, preventing him from seeing the seriousness of the problem. Having eliminated the doctrine of forms and the active intellect, he is left with a gap between the mechanistic explanation of the senses and the understanding. That the gap between the purely corporeal imagination and the purely spiritual mind is bridged he has no doubt, but no coherent explanation is given of how this happens. Figure, unlike the scholastic forms, cannot exist in an immaterial mind.

The *Rules*: Seeds of Future Problems

Although in the *Rules* Descartes does not introduce the methodic doubt that in his later works makes our knowledge of the external world problematic, certain aspects of the theory of perception presented in the *Rules* could logically lead to the view that our knowledge of the external world is indirect. Once the cognitive power has been reified and made a separate thing from the imagination and common sense, the cognitive power confronts something that is fundamentally other than itself. The imagination and the images in it confront the mind as an object. Thus the imagination is the focal point for these problems, since it is the point of contact between the cognitive power and the corporeal images conveyed from the external senses. As such, it is essential to explain how the understanding is enabled to know corporeal things—either our own body or external objects. Descartes himself says in Rule XII, "If, however, the intellect proposes to examine something which can be referred to the body, the idea of that thing must be formed as distinctly as possible in the imagination. In order to do this properly, the thing itself which this idea is to represent should be displayed to the external senses."[51]

Leaving aside the question of whether what is formed in the imagination is an "idea" or a purely corporeal image, we note that it "represents" the thing itself. The mind's contact with the world is via the imagination. Therefore, as Descartes notes later in Rule XII, we could easily be deceived if our imagination is diseased. In order to avoid error, he says, the "wise man will judge that whatever comes to him from his imagination is really depicted in it, [but] he will never assert that it passes, complete and unaltered, from the external world to his senses, and from his senses to the corporeal imagination, unless he already has some other grounds for claiming to know this."[52]

The obvious question that Descartes does not pose at this point is that if our only contact with the world is via ideas or images in the imagination, how can we *ever* tell how well they represent things outside of us? Although any theory of perception must account for the fact that a malfunctioning body can cause perceptual errors, Descartes' sharp dualism makes this problem particularly intransigent, especially since he has eliminated the "forms" that served as a kind of bridge between intellect and world and left the mind confronting figures traced in the imagination—and these are clearly something physical. Thus, the danger that our knowledge of the world will come to be regarded as indirect is particularly serious for Descartes.

In addition to the problems of connecting his mechanistic account of the senses with the incorporeal cognitive power and the danger that the ideas/figures in the imagination might emerge as some sort of representational entities between the knowing power and the object, Descartes also must deal with our perception of qualities if his theory is to win out over the scholastic one. To do this, he must develop a consistently mechanistic account of the objects of vision, namely light and color, and he sets out to do this in the *Dioptrics*.

2

Descartes' Theory of Light and Color

GIVEN DESCARTES' GOAL OF PROVIDING A THOROUGHLY MECHANISTIC AC-count of vision, he must develop this first for the objects of sight—namely light and color. His theory of light and color is in some ways still within the Aristotelian tradition. Like Aristotle he rejects theories either that objects give off little copies of themselves or that the eye emits visual rays.[1] He also remains within the Aristotelian tradition in his belief that colors are modifications of pure light and are to be arranged on a scale from strong to weak.[2] And both hold that our perception of light and color results from a kind of action of the intervening medium, but they understand that action in very different ways. Descartes' commitment to mechanism leads him to make deep changes that undercut Aristotelian realism about color. Nonetheless, one should beware of too quickly attributing to Descartes the kind of idealistic view of colors found, for example, in Nicolas Malebranche, who takes colors to be mental in nature and identifies them with ideas or sensations in our mind. Certainly the roots of this view are to be found in Descartes, but so are several other views about the nature of colors.

As a preliminary to Descartes' account of light and color, I first provide some historical background. Since Descartes' scholastic opponents were (in a general way at least) within the Aristotelian tradition in their understanding of light and color, I begin with relevant passages from Aristotle and briefly summarize some of the most important intervening developments. I then look at Descartes' own explanatory framework and the constraints this necessarily places upon his theory of light and color. Finally, I consider in more detail the question of the ontological status of colors.

Historical Background

ARISTOTLE ON LIGHT AND COLOR

Aristotle's discussion of light and color is rather brief and cryptic. He begins by noting that the object of sight is the visible, and what is visible is color (*DA*,

418a26–34). However, colors can be seen only in the presence of light, and thus Aristotle begins his discussion with light and its relation to the medium (the diaphanous). There are in nature, Aristotle says, some things that are transparent, and these are not visible in themselves, but owe their visibility to the color of something else (*DA*, 418a4–6)—we do not see them; we see through them. Air, water, crystal, and various other things to a lesser extent share this common transparent (or translucent or diaphanous) nature. The transparent, however, can only serve as a vehicle for color when it is illumined by light. Light, Aristotle says, is the activity of the transparent. The transparent also possesses the potentiality of the contrary—darkness (*DA*, 418b8–11). He also states: "Light is as it were the proper color of what is transparent, and exists whenever the potentially transparent is excited to actuality by the influence of fire or something resembling the uppermost body" (*DA*, 418a11–14). He even refers to light once as the "soul" of the diaphanous medium.

Thus, Aristotle is freed from the idea that light is material. If it were material, he says, it could not be in the same place as the diaphanous medium, since two things cannot be in the same place at once. In seeing light as an act of the transparent medium, he is also freed from the notion that it travels necessarily in a sequential way through successive parts of space, arriving first at the midpoint between object and eye (as is true of sound and odor). Light, he says, is not a local motion, but rather a qualitative change, and this sort of change can conceivably take place in a thing all at once, just as water may freeze simultaneously in all its parts. Even though parts of water *may* freeze sequentially if it is a large body of water, the same is not true of light, as he states clearly in *De Sensu* 446b26–447a12.[3] All parts of the medium are affected at once when it is in contact with fire or a celestial body. This is confirmed by his remarks in the *Nichomachean Ethics* 1174a15 and b12 to the effect that vision is perfect at any instant and involves no temporal process.

Once the diaphanous medium has become actualized by the presence of fire or the celestial body (the necessary first step in the visual process), it is then capable of being further actualized or moved by the colors of objects in such a way that these colors are communicated to the eye. Aristotle's remarks in the *De Anima* on the subject of color are quite brief. It is of color that visibility is predicated essentially (418a30). Color is able to move the already actualized transparent medium (419a12–15). Color "sets in movement not the sense organ but what is transparent, e.g. the air, and that, extending continuously from the object of the organ, sets the latter in movement" (419a12–16). The impression given is that color is in some sense a property of things overlying their surfaces, yet very little is said about what colors are in the object. Instead, Aristotle explains how they affect the diaphanous medium and the sense organ.

In the *De Sensu* this gap is filled in to some extent, and colors in the objects themselves are connected with the existence of the translucent element in them. "It is therefore the translucent, according to the degree to which it subsists in bodies (and it does so in all more or less), that causes them to partake of color" (439b8–10). And thus it must figure importantly in our definition of color: "We may define color as the limit of the translucent in a determinately bounded body" (439b12), "color being actually either *at* the external limit, or being *itself* that limit in bodies" (439a30).

Aristotle then proceeds to draw a rather interesting connection between light and color:

> That which, when present in air produces light may be present also in the translucent which pervades determinate bodies; or again, it may not be present, but there may be a privation of it. Accordingly, as in the case of air the one condition is light, the other darkness, in the same way the colors white and black are generated in determinate bodies. (439b14–18)

The other colors, Aristotle believes, arise from a mixture of white and black (442a12–14), there being a finite number of species of colors (440b24–5).

Although Aristotle's account of light and color is not very carefully worked out, a few things do emerge from it clearly. The diaphanous medium is the key to understanding both light and color, for light is the act of that medium, and color involves it also in two ways. The medium conveys the forms of colors to the eye, and the translucent element is present to some degree in all bodies and accounts for the colors of those bodies. Aristotle is a realist about colors; he believes that bodies are in fact colored. Colors exist actually at the surfaces of bodies (and only potentially in their interior) and thus have the power to actualize the medium (which has already been actualized by light). But the way in which colors are conveyed to the eye must not be interpreted as a local motion, but rather as a qualitative change.

INTERVENING DEVELOPMENTS

Between Aristotle and Descartes lie centuries of important work in optics by the Greeks and the Arabs as well as by those in the Latin West who, in the wake of the influx of ancient and Arabic texts in the twelfth and thirteenth centuries, attempted to integrate the earlier traditions and develop an adequate theory of vision.[4] No sharp dividing line existed between philosophy and natural science during this period, and by the seventeenth century, the long tradition of commentaries on Aristotle's *De Anima*, *De Sensu*, and *Meterology* had broadened out to include material from the perspectivist tradition—a tradition that had its roots in the work of the great Arab mathematician Alhazen and that combined his view that each point on the visible object radiates light in all directions independently of all other points with a basically Aristotelian understanding of the nature and propagation of light and with some Neoplatonic elements such as the theory of emanation.

For the purposes of the present discussion of Descartes' theory of light and color, I focus on the work of writers who were or might have been familiar to Descartes and on their understanding of the role of the medium in vision, since this is essential to understanding light and color. Descartes was certainly exposed to the work of the perspectivists, most importantly through his reading of Johannes Kepler, whom he refers to in a letter as "mon 1er maistre en Optique,"[5] and whose work was heavily indebted to the perspectivist tradition.[6] In addition to Kepler, he also read such other perspectivists as Witelo and probably was at least familiar with Alhazen and John Pecham, although probably not Roger Bacon.[7]

In addition to his reading of books specifically on optics, of course, Descartes was exposed to a number of commentaries on Aristotelian works and to textbooks that summarized scholastic philosophy (such as Eustace of St. Paul). These remained within a generally Aristotelian framework, in that they took colors to be real qualities of objects and treated light and color in the medium in qualitative terms. They did, however, differ from Aristotle in treating not only color but also light as essentially (or per se) visible. A distinction between *lux* and *lumen* was widely accepted, with *lux* being light as it exists in luminous bodies and *lumen* being light as it exists diffused in the medium. Light is neither matter nor motion, but a qualitative state whose cause is an inherent attribute of luminous bodies. *Lux* has the power to produce qualitative changes in the transparent medium; its form is replicated as *lumen* in all directions. *Lumen* is the physical form or species of *lux*.[8] It was widely believed that light was propagated instantaneously, being a qualitative change that occurs all at once throughout the medium (as Aristotle had held), although some held that it took some imperceptibly small amount of time.

One area in which Aristotle's commentators developed his thought was in trying to explain how the species of light and colors exist in the medium. Aristotle said very little about this, beyond that they involved a qualitative change in the medium, and his successors attempted to say more about the nature of these qualitative changes. The reason why they found it necessary to do this was because they were puzzled about why it is that if person A is looking at a red object while person B looks at the medium between the object and the perceiver A, the medium does not appear red to B. In what sense, then, is the medium informed with the form of redness? Aquinas notes that these forms, or "species" as he calls them,[9] are not present in the medium in the same sort of way they are present in the object (the hylomorphic model), but rather have an "intentional existence" in the medium.[10]

The terms *species* or *intentional species*, then, came to be used by most scholastics (except those who followed Ockham in rejecting the notion of species entirely),[11] but not everyone agreed about what was meant by species or intentional species. A number of different positions were held, with correspondingly different explanations of the fact that the medium itself does not appear to be colored. Averroes, for example, in *Epitome of Parva Naturalia Treatises*, argued that the reason we could not perceive the species in the medium was because "the existence of forms in the medium is of a kind intermediate between the spiritual and the corporeal."[12]

Many followers of St. Thomas were also willing, although in a different way from Averroes, to spiritualize the species in the medium. They reasoned that in order to produce a spiritual immutation in the sense organ, the sensible species must possess a kind of intentional being in the medium. And this was frequently accounted for by the spiritualizing effect of light. Light could spiritualize the species or enable the object to exercise intentional causality because it was, itself, the intentional presence in the medium of the celestial bodies and the separated substances.[13] This sort of thinking resulted in a number of difficulties when it came to connecting intentional being with natural being, or intentional causality with natural causality, and there was a tendency among later Thomists to sharply separate intentional being and natural (or corporeal) being (although the two were supposed to be in some way parallel). Cardinal Cajetan, for example, says, "There are two kinds of beings. Some are created primarily in order to exist, though perhaps secondarily they may represent others: these we call things (*res*). Others are primarily created in order to represent others: we call these intentions of things, and species—either sensible or intelligible."[14]

Jesuits such as Suarez were highly critical of the doctrine of intentionality held by Cajetan and other Thomists.[15] Ruvio, for example, whose work may well have influenced Descartes,[16] argues that species in the medium have a purely corporeal being. He says,

> Sensible species have a corporeal existence, not a spiritual existence. At the same time, their existence is not a natural corporeal existence, but one which is very much degenerate compared to natural existence. That is why it is called "intentional"— indeed it is a kind of diminished existence and one which is far inferior to the natural existence of the object. For that reason [sensible species] are not sensible, although they are the means by which the object is sensed.[17]

Descartes' response to these sorts of metaphysical disputes over the ontological status of species or sensible qualities in the medium is to reject the notions of species or intentional species altogether and to attempt a wholly mechanistic account of what occurs in the medium. Indeed, he has to, since he has rejected the whole metaphysics of form and matter and the notion of formal causality that are built into the concept of species.

One thing that has puzzled commentators, however, is that when Descartes discusses intentional species he seems to have in mind something like the eidola of the Epicureans.[18] This is certainly not the Thomist theory.[19] Gilson suggests Eustace of St. Paul as a possible source of Descartes' non-Thomistic understanding of them.[20] Gilson notes that although Eustace's definition of intentional species is a Thomist one, he does say things about them that could easily give rise to confusion.[21] Given the diverse character of seventeenth-century scholastic thought, however, Descartes could have come in contact with any number of writers who lapsed into thinking of intentional species in this way, or at least spoke of them in careless ways that might allow such a reading. For while species were held to be accidents and not substances by virtually all the scholastics, there was a general tendency, particularly among writers of textbooks and manuals, to think of them more in terms of images rather than abstract concepts. As Reif puts it: "The conceptual distinctions with which their highly abstract analysis terminates begin to be imagined as things,"[22] and this resulted in a strong tendency to reify species.[23]

Whether Descartes believes he is attacking a serious and widely held theory when he talks about the species that fly through the air is not clear. He could, of course, be trying to caricature his opponents. But in any case, it is quite clear that he wishes to materialize what occurs in the medium and eliminate all talk of "intentional species." In this his view resembles that of the Jesuits, like Ruvio, who held that species in the medium have a purely corporeal being, although Descartes' view is more radical than theirs in that it eliminates formal causality and eschews such central Aristotelian notions as act and potency and matter and form. There does, however, seem to be a common concern to keep the lines of demarcation between the spiritual and the material sharp by treating everything outside the mind in strictly materialistic terms.

Descartes, then, was impatient with the metaphysical disputes engaged in by scholastic philosophers. He disagreed radically with the Aristotelian understanding of *what* is transmitted through the medium, rejecting species and the Aristotelian metaphysical notions built into the notions of species (such as formal causality) and substituting mechanical pressure for formal change. Nonetheless, he is actually heavily indebted to his scholastic predecessors in the perspectivist tradition for his understanding of the physical act of light radiation.[24] Like them he accepted a view of the universe as a plenum, saw light radiation as an exercise of power generated at a luminous surface, regarded rays as mathematical fictions, employed the real/virtual distinction to treat the medium as both continuous and discontinuous, denied action at a distance, and treated light atomistically and mechanistically without claiming it to be actual matter in motion.[25] The idea of treating light by analogy with projectile motion was not original with Descartes, and it could be argued that he merely literalized the mechanistic implications present in the work of his perspectivist predecessors, although he doubtless read them through a mechanistic mindset and overlooked those aspects of their theories which did not fit with his.[26]

In sum, Descartes' attempt to provide a mechanistic account of light and color did not emerge out of a vacuum. While the perspectivists remained broadly Aristotelian in their understanding of light, Descartes was able to build on already existing mechanistic elements in their theory of light. And although colors as they existed in the medium were spoken of as "sensible forms" or "species," there was widespread dissatisfaction with the term *species* and a desire to eliminate it.[27] There was also a general interest in mechanistic explanations, and at least some of those arguing about sensible species (e.g., Ruvio) took the position that there was no such thing as intentional being outside the mind and therefore treated species in the medium as purely corporeal. The originality of Descartes' theory lies in the fact that he swept away more of the scholastic conceptual apparatus and tried be more ruthlessly mechanistic than his predecessors.

I turn now to consider briefly the metaphysical and methodological assumptions with which Descartes approaches his study of light and color.

Descartes' Explanatory Framework: Mechanism and Models

While Descartes, like the Aristotelians, believes that light is to be explained by the action of the intervening medium and that no matter need pass from the object to the eye, his commitment to a mechanistic view of nature requires him to treat the action of that medium very differently from the way they do. And his account of light is shaped not only by the requirements of a mechanistic physics but also by the fact that he regards the use of models or analogies as important and even indispensable in physics.

That Descartes, as a practicing scientist, is firmly committed to mechanism is generally conceded. This means, for one thing, that he is committed to a methodology that permits recourse only to certain sorts of explanatory principles in physics. Eduard Dijksterhuis characterizes this methodology as follows: "Cartesian physics . . . is mechanistic in character. This implies that it uses no explanatory principles other than the concepts employed in mechanics: geometric concepts such as size, shape, quantity, which are used by mechanics as a department of mathematics, and motion which forms its specific subject."[28]

Mechanism thus places various constraints on how vision could be explained. Since there is no void or action at a distance, light is explained in terms of the pressure that luminous bodies exert upon the air particles, which in turn press against the eye. Colors are explained in terms of the spinning motions of light particles, the nerves explained in terms of pushing or pulling a semi-rigid body, etc. There is no essential difference between the way the body functions and the way inanimate objects do; the principles of mechanics are applied equally to both. Mechanism, however, can also be viewed as a metaphysical position that:

> recognizes as actually existing in nature only those things which can be described and explained by means of these concepts. It not only excludes all notions of animation, internal spontaneity and purpose, but it also denies all internal change in the particles of matter . . . it also banishes from physics all secondary qualities of matter.[29]

One could, in principle, subscribe to a mechanistic methodology in science while maintaining a sort of agnosticism about the real natures of the things and processes thus explained. Descartes, himself, sometimes seems to be doing this. He assures the reader that he is merely showing that it is *unnecessary* to postulate substantial forms, real qualities, etc., that he can explain the phenomena of nature without them, but that he is not *denying* their existence. There is, however, every reason to suppose that these disclaimers are politically motivated and no reason to suppose that Descartes was genuinely agnostic about the nature of the physical world.

Descartes' mechanism, however, is given something of an idiosyncratic twist by his commitment to the use of models or analogies as a way of explaining phenomena. This is a deep and persistent aspect of his thought and not just a way of avoiding the controversies that raged around Galileo.[30] The kind of models he seeks to develop are ones that explain microscopic phenomena by analogy with medium-sized objects readily accessible to the senses. Descartes strongly defends this sort of explanation. In a letter to Morin in 1638, he says, "I claim that they [models and analogies] are the most appropriate way available to the human mind for explaining the truth about questions in physics; to such an extent that, if one assumes something about nature which cannot be explained by any analogy [*comparaison*] I think that I have conclusively shown it is false."[31]

In light of Descartes' stated intention to eschew all merely probable opinions and "never [to] receive for true, anything which I do not know evidently to be such,"[32] his pervasive reliance on comparisons and analogies is puzzling. One function of his models is certainly to make his theories intelligible to popular audiences. This, however, cannot be their only purpose since the models also appear in works not intended for popular audiences.[33] Given how strongly he defends this practice, it seems unlikely that he regards them as only a temporary expedient, to be replaced as soon as possible by an explanation that does not involve models. A given model may, of course, be superseded by a better one, but the necessity of using such models will not disappear. He did not just have recourse to such models out of desperation because the mathematics required to describe physical reality had become too difficult for him.[34]

Why, then, does Descartes rely so much on models? Perhaps the deepest reason has to do with his view of the role of the imagination in our knowledge of nature, as he develops it in the *Rules,* particularly Rules XII and XIV. When the intellect acts alone, he tells us, it is free of images or "bodily representations."[35] But when the intellect "proposes to examine something which can be referred to the body, the idea of that thing must be formed as distinctly as possible in the imagination."[36] Sometimes this can be effected by presenting the thing itself to our senses, so that its idea will be transmitted to the imagination, but the intellect can also act directly on the imagination "in order to form new figures."[37]

Not only is the imagination useful in physics, but it is necessary, since the pure intellect by itself can grasp only abstract entities like number or magnitude, which are in themselves indeterminate and thus bear no relation to the world. The imagination is required to represent abstract entities symbolically, thus rendering them determinate. Thus in the *Discourse*, he symbolically represents the object of universal mathematics as lines, and in the *Rules,* he compares differences between colors with the relationships between various lines and planes.[38] If the imagination is essential to our knowledge of the world, this would account for Descartes' reliance on models—for models are just those imaginative constructions that we must rely on in order to understand the corporeal world.[39]

Given, then, that some sort of imaginative models are necessary, how does Descartes go about constructing such models? One of his clearest explanations of his procedure is found in *Principles*, Part IV, 203, where he discusses how we can know the shapes and motions of imperceptible particles. First of all, he considers what clear and distinct ideas he has and notes that these include sizes, shapes, and motions, and the "rules in accordance with which these three things can be modified by each other."[40] Then he considers the various ways in which sizes, shapes, and motions could interact to produce the effect he is trying to explain. Since he has observed how the interaction of perceptible bodies produces certain effects, he reasons that the same causes operate also on a more minute level. Being guided by the analogy between natural processes and artifacts, he then tries to track down the imperceptible causes that account for the effects we perceive. Thus his models will necessarily be mechanistic in nature and involve analogies with ordinary medium sized objects perceptible by our senses.

I turn, now, to examine his theory of light and the way in which he employs models and analogies. I will then be in a position to reflect more about the implications of his use of models and the shortcomings of this method.

Light

Descartes' mechanistic theory of light was, he believed, central to his physics. Inasmuch as it provided the foundation for his attempted mechanization of colors, it was particularly important to his attack on his scholastic Aristotelian opponents (as discussed in the Introduction). His treatise on physics, *The World*, is subtitled *Treatise on Light*. In *The World* he develops an elaborate sort of fable—a cosmological account of the origin of the world, the development of the three elements, and an explanation of what light is based upon this theory. He is careful to present this theory as a fable—an account of how things *might* have come to be, at least partly because he believes it conflicts with the Church's doctrine of creation.

In the *Dioptrics,* Descartes again returns to the subject of light, but this time he does not claim to give us the real nature of light, but only to provide us with some useful models for explaining the observed behavior of light, and offers us three different models. Although the physics of *The World* does seem to underlie these models, the fit between the two works is sometimes rather loose.[41] I begin my discussion of light with *The World* since this work contains Descartes' basic physics of light.

THE WORLD

To start with, Descartes says, let us assume that God created the universe completely full of uniform matter, in particles of roughly equal size, and endowed them with motion—turning about their own centers and moving also in circles around numerous centers or vortices. Given only this, then, Descartes claims that he can account for all the observed phenomena of nature—a striking contrast with Aristotle's emphasis upon the qualitative differences between elements and upon forms as being the specifying principle of things—a role which must be played by motion for Descartes.

Since the particles have slight differences in their size and different situations with regard to the centers of the vortices, they eventually go through a series of mechanically produced changes to form the three major elements. The smallest and fastest moving particles wind up closer to the center of the vortices, the heaviest and slowest moving ones, being composed of irregularly shaped particles, stick together and form solid bodies moving around the center, while the middle-sized particles fill the spaces in between. Of the third element, the one that forms solid bodies, we need not say much. It is described as the opaque element since solid bodies reflect light, and all the objects we see are mainly composed of this element. The first and second elements are those most involved in Descartes' explanation of light.

The first element is comprised of the smallest and fastest moving particles that have come to be concentrated at the center of the vortices. It is described as luminous and is found in its unmixed form in the sun and fixed stars. Fire, as we find it on earth, is a mixed form of the first element. Descartes describes it as follows:

> In order not to be forced to admit any vacuum in nature, I will not attribute to it parts which have any determinate size or figure, but I am persuaded that the impetuosity of its motion is sufficient to cause it to be divided in all ways and senses by impact with other bodies and its parts change their shape at all moments to accomodate that of the places into which they enter.[42]

It is not entirely clear here whether he is saying that the size and shape of these particles changes constantly, or that they have no determinate size and shape at all. If he means the latter, this would cause problems with a physics that purports to explain all the phenomena of nature in terms of the location, motion, and shape of the small parts of matter. In any case, it is the function of the first element to move rapidly about and fill up the gaps between the larger particles of the other two elements, so that no matter is wholly without some admixture of the first element.

The second element is composed of particles that are completely smooth and rounded like pebbles on the beach, since all the rough edges have been broken off in the course of swirling around the vortices. There are always tiny spaces between them to be filled up by the first element, and so the second element is never without some of the first element. This applies both to the heavens, where we find the second element (which he characterizes as the "transparent") in its pure form, and to the earth, where we find the more gross and mixed form of the air.[43]

Luminous bodies, such as the sun, are composed entirely of the pure first element. They are round, perfectly liquid, and subtle. "[They] turn without ceasing much faster and in the same direction as the particles of the second element which surround them. [They] have the ability to increase the motion of those to which they are closest, and even to push them in all directions, and this by an action which I must soon explain as clearly as I can."[44] This action, he then goes on to say, is what we call light. Light is, thus, a kind of pressure, a *tendency* to move that is transmitted by the second element particles. This tendency, of course, involves no will or thought on the part of the particles, but is merely a disposition to move, which is present even though the surrounding bodies may prevent it from actually moving.[45]

In retreating away from the center around which they revolve, the second element particles tend away from the center along straight lines. This is the case because even though the second element particles are not all lined up in straight lines, they do touch each other. Thus the action or pressure we call light is transmitted instantaneously over any distance. Light, as it exists in the world, then, is a sort of pressure, action, tendency, or inclination to move transmitted by the second element particles, and not a material thing. There is no actual movement, only the tendency.

Even in *The World,* however, Descartes feels the need to bring in the model of the little moving balls (which does involve actual motion) when he tries to explain reflection and refraction and refers the reader to the *Dioptrics* for a fuller explanation.

THE *DIOPTRICS*

Descartes' purpose in the *Dioptrics,* he tells us, is to discuss light only insofar as its rays enter the eye, are reflected and refracted by various bodies, etc., and thus, it is not necessary for him to undertake to tell us the real nature of light. He thus falls back on his method of providing us with models or comparisons to help us understand light:

> It will suffice that I make use of two or three comparisons which help to conceive it in the manner which to me seems the most convenient to explain all those of its properties that experience acquaints us with, and to deduce afterwards all the others which cannot be so easily observed; imitating in this the astronomers, who, although their assumptions are almost all false or uncertain, nevertheless, because these assumptions refer to different observations which they have made, never cease to draw many very true and well-assured conclusions from them.[46]

He then presents us with three models to help us understand the nature of light: the blind man's stick, the vat of grapes, and the moving projectile.

The Blind Man's Stick

The first analogy given in the *Dioptrics* is the familiar analogy of a light ray with the stick a blind man uses to feel objects. This comparison was given in *The World*, where the second element particles that touch each other play the part of the stick, although they are not actually joined together.[47] Again, light is described as a kind of "movement or action, very rapid and lively, which passes toward our eyes through the medium of the air and other transparent bodies."[48] What is occurring is just like what occurs with the blind man's stick, where the movement or resistance of the bodies he touches with one end of his stick is transmitted instantly to the other end. The sun's rays, thus, extend from the sun to us in an instant.

Descartes' use of the stick analogy in the *Dioptrics* goes further than his use of it in *The World* in that he suggests it can also explain our perception of color. We perceive colors by means of light. In fact he actually says that "colors are nothing else, in bodies that we call colored, than the diverse ways in which these bodies receive light and reflect it against our eyes."[49] Our seeing different colors, then, is compared to the blind man's feeling the difference between mud, water, and sand. These differences are perceived because of the ways the object moves or resists the movements of the stick. From these rather hastily drawn comparisons, he concludes that we have no need to assume that anything material passes from the object to the eye, nor that anything in the objects is similar to the ideas or sensations we have of them and triumphantly announces that we are thus "delivered from all those small images flitting through the air called 'intentional species' which have so troubled the minds of the philosophers."[50]

On closer examination, however, the picture is not as clear as Descartes would like us to believe. There are obvious disanalogies between light and the blind man's stick, as he himself notes a few sentences later, and it is not clear that he has fully abandoned the idea that there is some sort of emission from luminous bodies that travels to the eye. He speaks, for example, of objects "receiving and reflecting light." This latter point will become clear especially when we look at the third analogy he gives for light.

Descartes himself notes the obvious disanalogies, and in attempting to resolve them, he says some rather startling things, such as that "objects of sight can be felt, not only by means of the action which, being in them, tends towards the eyes, but also by means of that which, being in our eyes, tends toward them."[51] This statement occurs in the context of Descartes' trying to work out the disanalogies between light and a stick, for inasmuch as he referred above to the "movement and resistance" of objects, it is clear that there can be no resistance unless the stick is pressed against the object instead of being wholly passive, and how can this be transposed to our account of vision? At this point, he suggests that there can be a certain action proceeding from eye to object, as happens with cats who can see in the dark, although this does not happen with "ordinary men."[52] Seeming to realize he is on thin ice here, he concedes that, after all, the analogy between air and the stick is imperfect, so we must make use of another comparison, and he moves on to his second analogy.

The Vat of Grapes

The second comparison for explaining what light is like is illustrated in figure 2.1. The grapes being pressed for wine are densely packed, but a fluid fills in all the spaces between them. If a hole is opened at the bottom, all of the parts of the wine tend immediately to descend towards A in straight lines. If two holes are opened, say A and B, the parts of the wine at D tend toward both of these holes at the same time. The parts of the wine at E and C also tend toward both holes,

Figure 2.1

and the important thing here is that all these different lines of action do not interfere with each other even if they cross. Thus, this analogy is more apt than the stick analogy for explaining certain properties of light rays. If two sticks crossed they would obviously interfere with each other; the floating grapes do not interfere, even though, being supported by each other, they do not tend to descend and may even be moved in many ways by those who are pressing them. The parts of the wine at C tend toward B in straight lines, although they cannot actually move in straight lines because of the grapes in between, and tend toward both A and B although they cannot actually move in both directions at once. Light, also, must be taken as an "action" or tendency rather than as an actual movement.

This particular model of light is important to Descartes because it enables him to explain how the rays can cross without interference. One of his main accomplishments in the *Dioptrics* is, he says, to explain

> how the rays from several different objects can enter together into the eye, or coming toward different eyes, can pass through the same place in the air without intermingling or preventing each other or being disturbed by the fluidity of the air or the agitation of the winds . . . how this does not prevent them [rays] from being exactly straight.[53]

Just how the vat of grapes model connects to the physics of *The World* is unclear. Descartes compares the wine with the subtle fluid material that stretches from us to the stars, while the grapes are compared to the air or other transparent bodies.[54] This sounds as if it is the wine that represents the first element, and all in all this interpretation makes the most sense of this whole section. The wine tends towards the holes in the bottom of the vat, while the grapes simply float in it. But if we read him this way, it seems inconsistent with the analogy in which the air is compared to the stick—to that which transmits the action to our eyes. In *The World*, the second element (or air) particles transmit the action to our eyes, and *Treatise on Man* contains the same view.[55] Instead of attempting to reconcile these, Descartes instead moves on and presents a third analogy.

The Moving Projectile

Descartes' third model is in obvious tension with the previous two and if accepted would cause problems with the very difficulties Descartes is so confident that he has resolved with his previous models. It is brought in mainly to help him explain reflection and refraction. We are asked to think of light as being like little balls, or like a stream of little balls whose behavior can be explained by the same mechanical laws as those governing the behavior of moving projectiles. Just as a moving ball can lose its movement when it hits something soft, or be deflected by a hard surface, or acquire a spinning motion if it hits a rough surface, so also the light rays (now conceived of as streams of little moving balls) can lose their motion when they encounter certain surfaces (those we call black), or be reflected back in all directions (by those we call white), or acquire various spinning motions (which happens with bodies we call colored). Highly polished surfaces reflect the rays back without changing the order among the rays and thus can serve as mirrors. Just as a ball moving from air into water has its movement deflected, so light passing through different mediums is deflected. This model turns out to be very rich in theoretical and practical implications and enables Descartes to explain colors as well as reflection and refraction.

The problem, of course, is that this third model, unlike the first two, involves the actual movement of particles and not just a pressure or a tendency to move. It is clear Descartes wants to paper over this discrepancy, and he is constantly conjoining terms like "action or movement"[56]and "movement or tendency,"[57]as though these were really the same. Scott points out that:

> The parts of the subtle matter on that side of the sun which faces us tend to move in right lines toward our eyes without being hindered by the more solid particles. From this, argues Descartes, it is clear that nothing material passes from the luminous body to our eyes.
> But it is abundantly clear from his writings that Descartes was unable to abandon the emission theory and his explanation of the different properties of light and color is quite unintelligible upon any other assumption.[58]

Ronchi notes the inconsistency,[59] as does Alquié,[60] who says that for a motion to be slowed down, turned aside, etc., it must be a movement actually realized and not just a tendency to move. And in this case, Alquié notes, all the difficulties that Descartes' theory had avoided (with crossing rays, etc.,) will reappear. Why do the streams of little moving particles not interfere with each other, get blown off course by the wind, etc.?

For the third model to be consistent with the first two, the inclination to move equated with light in the first two models must follow the same laws as actual movement of projectiles, an assumption Descartes explicitly makes in the Discourse on refraction (the second), but which is highly questionable. In a letter to Mersenne, Pierre de Fermat raises the objection that an inclination to move need not obey the same laws as an actual motion, but Descartes brushes aside the objection, finding it clear and evident that it does, since whatever is in the act (movement) must be there in the potency.[61] It is hard to know how to interpret Descartes' puzzling use of scholastic terminology here, since he clearly rejects the Aristotelian metaphysics on which such terminology is based.[62]

Finally, it is highly questionable whether Descartes can admit "tendencies" or "inclinations" at all and remain a consistent mechanist. It appears necessary when explicating tendencies or inclinations to employ at some point counterfactuals of the form "x would move in a straight line if its movement were not blocked or impeded." And it could be argued that a strict mechanist is not entitled to rely on counterfactuals.

CRITICAL REFLECTIONS ON DESCARTES' THEORY OF LIGHT

Descartes' theory of light provides us with an interesting example of his methodological commitment to the use of models or analogies in physics and in particular to his use of analogies between the behavior of objects too small to observe and that of ordinary medium-sized objects perceptible by the senses, such as sticks, grapes, and tennis balls. This methodology is, on purely scientific grounds, open to some serious objections. The value of explanation by analogy is, for a start, highly suspect in physics, since there are always disanalogies as well.[63] It is not self-evident, certainly, that microscopic phenomena behave like scaled-down versions of macroscopic processes.[64] Indeed, as modern physics has shown us, quite different concepts may be applicable to the two sorts of phenomena,[65] and not all scientifically acceptable theories involve easily visualizable models. Very few do, in fact. Descartes' excessive reliance upon these sorts of models is arguably one of the main causes of the sterility of his scientific method.

Many critics have noted this. Wallace, for example, says that Descartes' "faith in his ability to reduce all physical phenomena to easily imaginable mechanical motions" is a "shortcoming" in his methodology.[66] Scott notes that Descartes' attempts to reduce bodily functions to easily imaginable mechanical motions "led him to make almost every mistake it was possible to make."[67] Gaukroger also makes the point that Descartes' insistence on having models constructed out of notions that are intuitively clear and distinct to us led him to make serious mistakes in physics, since important concepts in physics (such as Newton's concept of mass) are frequently ones that cannot be abstracted from perception and that are not intuitively clear to us. Clinging to intuitive concepts may, in fact, impede the development of physics.[68] And Clarke notes that Descartes' reliance on mechanical models drawn from ordinary experience prevented him from making the sort of progress in science that has flowed from subsequent more perfectly mathematical physics.[69]

Quite apart from its shortcomings from a scientific point of view, Descartes' reliance on models and analogies raises some troubling problems for his ambitions in physics. In light of his desire to develop a deductive and certain physics, it is puzzling that he appears so unconcerned about the apparent inconsistencies among his theories. Are we to take the "fable" presented in *The World* and the three models of light developed in the *Dioptrics* as hypotheses about the way that the world really is, or is their value merely an instrumental one?

All the issues raised by Descartes' use of models in his physics cannot be adequately addressed within the scope of this essay.[70] But on the basis of *The World,* the *Dioptrics,* and the *Meteorology,* a good case can be made for the presence of a strong instrumentalist strand in his thinking about models. For example, just before he presents his models of light, he says:

> It is not necessary that I undertake to say truly what its [light's] nature is; and I believe that it will be enough if I use two or three analogies [*comparaisons*] which help us understand it in a way which is most convenient to explain all its properties which experience acquaints us with, and to subsequently deduce all those other properties which cannot be so easily noticed; in this approach imitating astronomers who, although their assumptions are almost entirely false or uncertain, nevertheless, because they agree with various observations which they have made, do not fail to draw many very true and very certain conclusions from them.[71]

If we take his attitude towards his models to be that they are of instrumental or predictive value only, this would successfully account for the otherwise puzzling fact that he does not seriously try to reconcile the tensions between his models.

But this reading does pose problems for his ambitions in physics. Descartes is, after all, after truth and not just predictive success. And if, in fact, his models do turn out to be inconsistent with each other, then this would be fatal for his project of constructing a deductive physics, since any inconsistencies among them would indicate inconsistency in the principles they had been derived from. And, finally, it should be noted that a purely instrumentalist attitude toward his models would make him vulnerable to some of the same criticisms he levels against scholastic explanations. If the models are postulated ad hoc to explain particular phenomena without any serious attempt to harmonize them, then their explanatory value is really no better than that of the *virtus dormitiva* caricatured by Molière. Given any physical phenomenon, Descartes can dream up a fanciful Rube Goldberg-style mechanistic explanation tailored specifically to that phenomenon—a kind of mechanistic *virtus dormitiva*.[72]

Thus, instrumentalism cannot, for a number of reasons, be a satisfactory position for Descartes to adopt. And he was obviously unhappy himself with the fact that he had to begin the *Dioptrics* and *Meteorology* with assumptions instead of proving them starting from first principles. There are indications that he believed he *could* prove his assumptions,[73] although it is difficult to see how they could be deduced from first truths, and no such deductions were ever provided even for his most general assumptions at the beginning of the *Meteorology*—such as that things are composed of corpuscles and that there is no void. And imaginative models pose special problems within a deductive system, unless they are merely aids to our understanding and/or eliminable in principle from the system.[74]

In spite of these unresolved problems, Descartes' theory of light did effectively persuade people that light could be explained mechanistically, thus preparing the ground for a mechanistic account of colors—a task that was particularly important in his struggle against the scholastics.

Color

Descartes' explanation of color in the *Dioptrics* and *Meteorology* was, perhaps, the most influential and important part of his theory of vision. He was especially proud of his explanation of the rainbow, and there is evidence from his correspondence that he was writing a treatise on "the colors of the rainbow and certain other sublunar phenomena" in 1629 when he became inspired by the new vistas opening before him and laid it aside, resolving now to write a work explaining "all the phenomena of nature, that is to say the whole of physics."[75]

The general principle involved in his explanation of color is quite simple and is based on the third model for light. The little moving balls (which represent light) may travel in straight lines only, and they may also move around their own centers while they do so. Their spinning motion has a certain ratio to their forward motion, and it is this ratio that determines our sensations of color. When the spin of the particles greatly exceeds their forward motion, they generate our sensation of red, or yellow if the spin is a bit less. If the spin is less than the forward motion, we see blue, and if it is much less we see green. The fact that certain bodies are consistently seen to be red or blue is accounted for by the fact that they cause the light particles that are moving in straight lines only to spin also around their centers after being reflected off their surfaces, much as a tennis ball starts to spin when grazed by the racquet. This account of color clearly requires actual movement of particles, for otherwise it makes no sense to speak of the movement of the particles "before" and "after" they are reflected from the surface of the object. Our vision of color occurs, of course, only when the light rays focused on our retinae cause motions in the optic nerve that are transmitted to the brain and eventually the pineal gland, where they act upon the soul.

Although Descartes realizes that our perception of color involves a long causal chain, this does not settle completely for him the question of the nature of color. Having abandoned the Aristotelian assumption that colors are real qualities of the object—proper objects of sight, not reducible to such common objects of sense as figure and motion,[76] he is left with several possible answers to the question of what colors are. He can identify colors with the structural properties of the surfaces of the object that cause it to reflect light as it does or with the spinning motion of the light particles themselves, either of which allows them a certain existence independent of the perceiver. Or, he can take the idealist route and identify them simply with the sensations we have of them. In his optical writings, Descartes seems inclined to hold all three views at different times.

Among the passages that seem to support a realistic interpretation of colors is his discussion of visual errors at the end of Discourse VI of the *Dioptrics*. He says:

> Because we normally judge that the impressions which stimulate [*meuvent*] our sight come from the places towards which we have to look to sense them, we may easily be deceived when they happen to come from elsewhere. Thus those who are affected with jaundice or else who look through a yellow glass, or who are enclosed in a room where no light enters except through such glass, attribute this color to all the bodies they look at. And the person shut up in the dark room who I just described attributes to the white body [the opaque cloth or paper placed in the back of a dissected eye, through which light is let into an otherwise darkened room] the colors of objects outside because he directs his sight solely upon that body.[77]

The implication of this passage is clearly that it is incorrect to attribute the yellow color to the objects seen in the three cases cited. Also, since it is wrong to attribute the colors to the piece of opaque paper or cloth, it would seem to follow that it would be correct to attribute them to the objects outside the dark room.

As for what colors in objects are, Descartes says:

> The object V, which I suppose, for example to be red, that is to say that it is disposed to cause the little parts of this subtle matter, which have been pushed only in straight lines by luminous bodies, to move also around their centers after having come into contact with the object, and that their two movements have between them the proportion which is required to make us sense the color red. [78]

The property in the object that we call color is picked out in terms of the sensation it causes in us, but Descartes does not appear to doubt that there is some physical property out there that causes the objects to reflect light in the way they do. After all, on his theory there could be no explanation for an object's disposition to reflect light in a particular way other than the configuration and/or motions of the particles that make up that object. We can say, thus, that objects are colored in the sense that their surfaces have certain structural properties that account for the ways in which they reflect light, and although scientists have not yet adequately understood just what it is about the surfaces that accounts for their way of reflecting light, there are doubtless such properties and when we know them, we will then know what colors are.

In a letter to Henri Regius he suggests that colors are to be identified with the configurations of particles in the surfaces of objects: "When you treat of colors, I cannot see why you exclude blackness, since the other colors too are only modes. I would simply say 'blackness too is commonly counted as a color yet it is nothing but a certain arrangement, etc.'"[79] This kind of reductivist explanation of color gives colors a reality independent of the perceiver to some extent. It is important that the red object is the one that imparts a particular motion to the little particles of the subtle matter that were previously moving only in straight lines without spinning. If the light particles had already had a spinning motion typical of, say, blue, then after being reflected off the red object ("red" in the sense defined above), they would not acquire the spin necessary to make us see red, but perhaps some average motion—causing us to see, say, purple. Nonetheless the object would still be red. Descartes does not explicitly discuss colors perceived under unusual lighting, but this sort of reasoning would be consistent with at least a lot of what he does say.

The situation, however, is more complicated. For we speak of colors in cases where there are no objects present. Light is often spoken of as colored, and there are phenomena like, for example, the rainbow, which require additional explanation. In discussing these, Descartes tends to identify colors with the motions of the particles of subtle matter. In the sixth discourse of the *Dioptrics*, he says of colors that "their nature consists only in diversity of movement"[80] and cites as evidence the fact that we see a flash of light when struck in the eye (even in a dark place) and the existence and behavior of after images (which change color as they fade). Also in line with this interpretation is a passage in the *Meteorology* where he says, "The nature of the colors which appear towards F consists only in the fact that these parts of the subtle matter that transmit the action of light tend to turn with more force than they tend to move in a straight line."[81]

On the basis of these passages, it seems Descartes might answer the question about the nature of color by saying it is a certain type of motion in the particles of the subtle matter that transmit light to us. If one takes this as the central meaning of the term *color*, then one can call objects "colored" as I do above, but only in a derivative sense—namely, that, because of the configuration and motion of their parts, they impart these motions to white light when it is reflected off them. However, either of the definitions I have examined so far—that is (1) color is a configuration of the minute particles that make up the surface of the object, which causes it to reflect light in a particular way, or (2) color is itself this spinning motion—do preserve a sort of objectivity for colors.

There are, however, passages where Descartes is closer to an idealist position on the nature of color, the most important of which occur in the *Meteorology* in the section on the rainbow. He speaks there of the spinning motions of the light particles, saying, "Those which have a much stronger tendency to rotate cause the color red and those which have only a slightly stronger tendency cause yellow."[82] This would prevent us from equating colors with the motions of the light particles and leads us instead to see these motions only as causes of the colors that, then, are to be identified with the sensations caused by the spinning light particles.

Descartes also says:

I do not care for the distinction of the philosophers when they distinguish between real colors and false or apparent ones. For since all their real nature is that they appear, it seems to me a contradiction to say that they are false and that they appear. But I admit that shadow and refraction are not always necessary to produce them, and that the parts of bodies called colored can interact with the light to increase or decrease the spinning of these parts of the subtle parts of matter. [83]

This passage might seem to be consistent with the view that colors are to be identified with the spinning motions of the light particles; wherever we have that, we have color regardless of whether this spinning motion was caused by refraction (as in the case of the rainbow) or by the reflection of light from an object. Since Descartes is taking the rainbow as a paradigm case of color perception and treating our more ordinary perception of objects as a special case, it is not surprising that he would tend to see color as being somehow in the light particles. Thus he speaks of objects "called" colored, causing doubt about whether the objects really are colored.

There are, however, hints of a deeper idealism in this passage. The statement that "all their real nature is to appear" certainly seems to make of colors something subjective. An "appearance" after all must be an apearance *to* someone. Colors cannot be identified with the spinning motion of the light particles if "all their real nature is to appear," since without a perceiver there is no appearance. Descartes also seems to identify colors with their appearance to the perceiver in saying that they cannot appear and be false. If this is so, it would seem that after images (the yellow color seen by the jaundiced man, etc.) would all be true and, indeed, that all talk of our color perceptions being true or false at all would be ruled out.

It might be suggested that there is another possible theory about the nature of colors that we have omitted—namely, the Lockean one that they are powers in the objects to cause sensations in us.[84] Descartes' occasional use of the term *disposition* (e.g., in *Principles*, Part IV, 198–99, where he uses *dispositiones* in Latin and *disposée* in French) might appear to support this interpretation. These words, however, denote primarily the layout or spatial arrangement of a thing and not anything like *disposition* in the modern sense of a tendency or inclination having its source in some power inherent in the object. Certainly, if Descartes is to be consistent with his own mechanistic principles, he cannot allow any inner principles of action in matter other than the size, shape, motion, and spatial arrangement of its parts. Although he does sail rather close to the wind in some other cases, such as his description of light as a tendency or inclination to move (rather than an actual movement),[85] there is no reason to think that he views colors as dispositions in this sense (i.e., as a movement that would be realized but for the fact that something is blocking its path).[86]

Thus, in his optical writings, Descartes appears to waver between several different theories of color. His radical dualism has driven a wedge between our sense experience and the way the world really is—the latter being revealed by mechanistic science only. This leads to problems with understanding even what it might *be* for a statement such as "this rose is red" to be true. If "this rose is red" is true if and only if there is something out there in the rose exactly like my sensation, this would be impossible, since sensations are modes of my mind (although ones that necessarily involve the body), and of course, nothing mental or conscious could be in material substances.[87] But with the instinctive realism of a scientist, Descartes continues to apply color terms all along the causal chain—to objects, light, and our sensations. He might, perhaps, do so legitimately if he admitted that color terms apply differently to our sensations and to their contributing causes and distinguished the different senses in which objects, light, and sensations are colored. Or he might do as Malebranche does—equate colors with sensations and insist that things external to the mind are merely the causes of colors. But he does not make either of these moves in any clear way.

The same sorts of ambivalence about color in the scientific writings persist in Descartes' later remarks on the subject. He continues to be interested in what colors in objects are. In the Fourth Replies he says it "depends simply on the exterior surface of bodies."[88] Presumably, then, colors would depend on the spatial arrangements and movements of the minute particles at the exterior surfaces of the bodies. And in his late unfinished work, *Description of the Human Body (La description du corps humain)*, he speculates about the reason why the blood of all animals is red, providing an elaborate explanation involving the movements of various sorts of particles in the blood.[89]

Significant trends in Descartes' thought, however, push him gradually more in the direction of seeing colors as existing only in the mind, as the problem of what I call "externality perception" became increasingly serious for him. Why do we perceive colors as external to our minds at all, or as external to our brains, since the motions that act immediately upon the soul are in the brain? Already in the Sixth Replies, he assigns color sensations to the second grade of sensory response—which includes "all the immediate effects produced in the mind as a result of its being united with a bodily organ."[90] However, he suggests[91] that our assigning color to a stick outside of us is a result of judgment.

> As a result of being affected by this sensation of colour, I judge that a stick, located outside me, is colored; and suppose that on the basis of the extension of the color and its boundaries together with its position in relation to the parts of the brain, I make a rational calculation about the size, shape, and distance of the stick: although such reasoning is commonly assigned to the senses, . . . it is clear that it depends solely on the intellect.[92]

His clearest discussions of externality perception occur in the *Passions of the Soul (Les passions de l'âme)*. He is very struck by the fact that the motions occurring in our brains must "represent these objects to the soul."[93] Thus, he says, when we see a light, motions are set up in our brain that give the soul sensations. We then "refer these sensations to the subjects we suppose to be their causes."[94] He does not use the word *judgment*, but the assumption is still that we would experience qualities as in our brains or minds unless something intervened to change this. To the extent that Descartes comes more and more to see externality perception as a problem, this indicates that he is focusing more on colors as sensations in our minds and thus moving more in the direction of an idealistic view of colors. And his concession in *Comments on a Certain Broadsheet (Notae in programma quoddam)* that all our ideas of sensory qualities must be innate would seem to reinforce the mind dependent status of colors still more.[95]

Conclusion

Whatever the problems with the details of his theory of light and color from a scientific point of view, Descartes was eminently successful in sweeping away the Aristotelian realistic view of colors and in clearing the way for a mechanistic account of them. A wedge had been driven between the world as we experience it and the world as science tells us it is, and the gap thus created has only widened since then. His successors disputed whether colors were to be understood as configurations of figure and motion at the surfaces of objects, as a property of light, as a mental state in the perceiver only, or (with Locke) as a "power" in the objects. But the traditional view of colors was no longer considered.

Although I undertake a full scale discussion of the epistemological ramifications of Descartes' theory of vision after I examine the processes that occur within the perceiver, I note here that his theory of light and color does have implications for the issue of whether we are to think of our perceptual knowledge as direct or indirect. On the one hand, his analogy between light and the blind man's stick supports the view that our perception gives us direct access to objects. The blind man feels the object itself and not some image or copy of it; so we feel objects by means of the light rays that touch and press against our eyes. The moving projectile model, by contrast, involves particles that must take some time to travel and could be disturbed by winds or intervening objects. Being bombarded by particles originating at the object can thus less plausibly be regarded as a direct contact with the object. This is probably one reason why Descartes clung so tenaciously to the stick analogy in spite of its dubious compatibility with the projectile model he needs to explain colors.

His treatment of color, however, seems to pull in a different direction. The world full of colored objects that our senses reveal to us is so radically different from the account of what the world is really like provided by mechanistic science that it seems natural to think that our senses give us direct access only to something subjective. Our sensations or ideas become, as Berkeley put it, "terminated within themselves."[96]

In the next chapter, I consider how Descartes mechanizes the processes that occur within the perceiver and the way in which these explain our perception of light and color.

3

The Mechanics of Vision and
Our Perception of Light and Color

ONE OF DESCARTES' CRITICISMS OF THE ACCOUNTS OF PERCEPTION OFFERED BY
the scholastics is that they fail to specify in detail the actual mechanisms involved
in perception:

> It is necessary to beware of assuming that in order to sense, the mind needs to
> perceive certain images transmitted by the objects to the brain, as our philosophers
> commonly suppose; or at least the nature of these images must be conceived quite
> otherwise than as they do. For inasmuch as they (the philosophers) did not consider
> anything about these images except that they must resemble the objects they represent,
> *it is impossible for them to show us how they can be formed by these objects, received
> by the sense organs, and transmitted by the nerves to the brain.*[1] (Emphasis added)

Building upon his mechanistic account of light and color, which explains how
it is that particles of subtle matter with various motions (spinning motions and
forward motions) arrive at the eye, Descartes goes on in *Treatise on Man* and the
Dioptrics to extend his theory to explain the process of perception all the way
from the formation of the retinal image to the merging of the two retinal images
at the pineal gland. The account given in these works grows out of the one he
developed in the *Rules*, but with one difference. The faculty psychology that still
lingered in the earlier work is eliminated; the common sense and the imagination
are telescoped together and hypothesized to be located at the pineal gland.

In this chapter, I discuss Descartes' account of the process of vision beginning
with the formation of the retinal image and ending with the formation of the
image (pattern of motions) at the surface of the pineal gland. It is not necessary
to go any further back than the work of Kepler in discussing the historical
background for Descartes' ideas about the formation of the retinal image, since
it was Kepler who first succeeded in explaining this correctly, and Descartes
simply took over Kepler's account. Aristotle knew very little about the nature
and function of the visual system; he was unaware of the existence and function
of the retina and wrongly saw sensation as a function of the vascular system.
While his mistaken belief that the heart was the central organ of sensation had

been corrected well before Descartes' time, it was not until Kepler that the role of the retina in vision and the formation of the retinal image were finally understood correctly.

An extensive historical discussion of the developments in the physiology of vision would also be of limited value, although for different reasons. While physiology had made some progress during the Middle Ages and the Renaissance (although rather less than optics), the nature of the delicate and complex mechanisms involved in vision was still largely undiscovered. Aristotle realized that there were channels leading inward from the eyes, and the existence of the optic nerves and their joining at the optic chiasma had been known for a long time before Descartes. Aquinas, for example, in his commentary on Aristotle's *De Sensu*, notes that the sensitive faculty is the "principle of the sensible operations which the soul exercises through the body" and that it must therefore be present in some definite body part. He thus suggests that the principle of vision is situated "in the environment of the brain where the two nerves coming from the eyes are joined." But his way of thinking about how vision occurs is still very much like that of Aristotle. He says, "The pupil is lighted up by an outside light, just as certain lamps are; therefore, when the passages of the eye which join the pupils to the principle of vision are severed, the light of this lamp cannot arrive at the principle of vision, and therefore vision is obscured."[2]

Kepler, with his superior knowledge of optics and physiology, exposed serious problems with any sort of account of vision involving light or species of light being transmitted into the brain but did not himself propose a solution to the question of what occurred beyond the retina. The field was thus left open to Descartes to do so. Descartes himself knew very little about the physiology of the visual system; what went on in the brain beyond the optic chiasma, or at least beyond the cerebral cavities to which he traced the optic nerves, was still largely unknown. Rough attempts had been made to correlate various functions with ventricles of the brain, but very little was really known about brain functions. In fact, Descartes does not incorporate even the work that *had* been done on the functions of the different parts of the brain, and the reason for this is philosophical. As Georges-Berthier puts it: "Descartes, dominated by his metaphysical idea of the absolute unity of the soul, does not bother to incorporate [the material on localization of cerebral functions] into his system" (translation mine).[3]

In order to bring into focus the philosophical issues involved in Descartes' physiology, I discuss his reasons for supposing that the pineal gland is the primary locus of the soul and that therefore the two retinal images must be merged there. He goes far beyond any physiological information available to him in postulating this second projection of the retinal images from the cerebral cavities to the pineal gland, and I examine his reasons for doing so. Interestingly, his method and some of his arguments are similar to those of Aristotle. In his more physiological treatises, Aristotle provides arguments for why the sensitive soul resides primarily in the heart, which are similar to those Descartes gives for selecting the pineal gland as the primary locus of the soul.[4] I therefore develop Descartes' arguments against the background of Aristotle's.

Having a far better understanding than Aristotle of the structure and function of the eye and the formation of the retinal image and having (in the interests of developing a completely mechanistic account of vision) replaced the Aristotelian notion of form with that of figure (see chapter 1), Descartes' theory encounters some serious problems, as I show in this chapter and the next one.

The Retinal Image

With Felix Platter's work the anatomy of the eye and the function of the retina had been correctly understood, and Kepler, building upon Platter's work and on his knowledge of mathematical optics, had at last come up with the correct explanation of the formation of the retinal image.[5] Thus, while Aristotle, having virtually no knowledge of the optical properties of the eye or the existence and function of the retina, had supposed that it was the watery part of the eye that received the forms of colors and conveyed them inward through the optic channels, Descartes could develop a theory of vision starting from his knowledge of the formation of the retinal image.

In many ways, the retinal image seems to be just what Descartes needs to make his theory of vision work. It provides a wonderful example of how the figure of the object is impressed upon the external sense, as he said in the *Rules*. According to Kepler's account, the rays from each point of the object are reunited (due to the refractive power of the lens) at a corresponding point on the retina, there tracing a reversed and inverted image of the object. Given Descartes' mechanistic theory of light and color, then, the rays impart motions to the retina in a way that can be seen as analogous to the way the seal impresses a pattern on the wax. Thus, a mechanistic analogue is provided for the Aristotelian notion of the sense receiving the forms or qualities of the object. As Descartes puts it in Rule XII: "The first opaque membrane in the eye receives the shape impressed upon it by the multicolored light."[6]

Descartes' account of the retinal image appears in the fifth discourse of the *Dioptrics*. Although it adds nothing to the theory developed by Kepler, it does raise some interesting philosophical issues. In order to convince the reader that a picture (*peinture*) of the objects we see is printed (*imprimé*) upon the back of the eye, Descartes describes an experiment that he, himself, performed.[7] He instructs the reader to take the eye of a cow or a newly dead man and to remove the back surface or retina leaving the rest of the eye as undisturbed as possible, to place a piece of opaque paper or egg shell behind it, and in a dark room to put

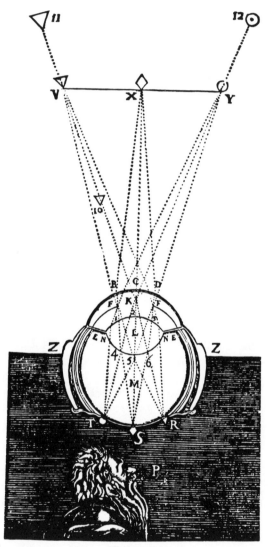

Figure 3.1

the eye in the hole of a specially made window that looks out on a brightly illuminated scene so that light enters only through the eye. The reader will then, he says, see appear on the paper a picture that represents all the objects in perspective.

Figure 3.1 illustrates the experiment, complete with the dark chamber and the man inside. Light travels from objects V, X, and Y, the light from each object being brought to a focus at a point on the opaque sheet of paper. If the light being reflected by object X is yellow, then as it shines through the paper it will cause us to see yellow at point S; if V is reflecting blue light, we will see blue at point R, and so also for Y (say it is red), and T. What appears on the paper will have the same colors in the same order as V, X, and Y, thus resembling them.

Although this little picture can be perfectly formed if all the conditions are right (the relevant conditions involve the shape of the lens, its distance from the retina, the width of the pupil, etc.), it nonetheless has certain imperfections. The principal one is that due to the way the eye is constructed, only those things brought to a focus near the center of the retina are seen clearly, while those toward the edges are very indistinct since the rays are not brought accurately to a focus. Thus the picture is clear only in the middle (we are, it should be remembered, still talking in terms of the man in the dark room looking at the back of the dissected eye). Other imperfections of the picture are that "its parts are reversed, that is to say in a position completely contrary to that of the objects; and . . . they [the parts] are elongated and shortened some more, some less, because of the differing distance and situation of the things which they represent, in the same way as in a perspective painting."[8] A small, close object occupies as much space as a larger, more distant one, and a straight line, VXY, is represented by a curved line, RST, due to the curvature of the eye.

This explanation of the retinal image and its manner of formation is indeed a convincing one, as the experiment is dramatic and easily visualizable. However, introducing the retinal image in this way could easily mislead an unwary reader into supposing that in vision the soul, like the man in the dark room, somehow gazes upon the pictures painted on the bottom of the eye—a view that would obviously lead to a vicious regress, since another eye would be needed with which to see the picture. The light rays may move the points on the retina, but no "picture" appears until the causal chain is broken, the retina replaced by an opaque white body, and another eye introduced.

Descartes himself is too sophisticated to fall into the error of supposing that we see our retinal images[9]—or at least not without a struggle. His struggle is evident when he says, "You see thus that although the soul has no need to contemplate any images which are similar to the things it senses, this does not prevent it from being true that the objects we look at imprint quite perfect ones [images] in the bottoms of our eyes."[10] The resembling images are thus almost an embarrassment to him, but this does not prevent him from relying on them in his explanation of vision.

The problem as Descartes understands it is how to transmit the retinal images to the brain, since he believes that the soul has its seat deep within the brain. This belief, in turn, is based on such evidence as the fact that damage or disease of the brain impedes sensation even though the rest of the body is intact, and damage to the nerves going from, say, the foot to the brain, prevents our having any sensations from the foot.[11] Aristotle, too, reasoning in a similar way, concludes that vision is not completed in the eye. From the fact that severing the passages leading inward from the eye causes blindness, he concludes that "the soul or its perceptive part is not situated at the external surface of the eye, but obviously somewhere within" (*DS*, 438b5–10).

The mode of transmission of the retinal image was perceived to be particularly problematic at the time Descartes was writing because, as Kepler points out, optics can do nothing to help us explain it. Optics, Kepler says, can take us only as far as the formation of a picture on the opaque surface of the retina, and what happens beyond this—whether the soul comes down to meet the images, or they are somehow transmitted to the seat of the soul or visive faculty—is something that must be left to the physicists or natural philosophers. He expresses opposition to Witelo's idea that "images of light" pass through the optic nerves on the grounds that these nerves follow crooked paths and go through dark places but does not himself offer a satisfactory alternative explanation. We must, Kepler says, leave it to the physicists or natural philosophers.[12]

Descartes' theory of color put him in a position to explain the transmission of the retinal image in a new way. The retinal image is a pattern of colored light focused upon the retina, and since colors are a function of the motions of the light particles, each color of light imparts a slightly different sort of motion to the nerves in that part of the retina upon which the light falls. The retinal image is thus, as it were, encoded into a pattern of motions structurally isomorphic with it, and these motions (unlike light itself) can be transmitted inward through the nerves.

Transmission of Retinal Image into the Cerebral Cavities

The nerves function to convey the image (i.e., the pattern of motions structurally isomorphic with the retinal image) inward from the eye. Each nerve, Descartes says, has three parts: (1) the outer sheath, which is like a hollow tube; (2) the threadlike fibers, which extend unbroken from the body part to the brain; and (3) the animal spirits, which flow through the tubes keeping them inflated so they do not pinch the little threads. The animal spirits are very fine particles, of the same type as the first element particles but having heat without light (unlike the first element particles that compose luminous bodies).[13] The little fibers convey motions to the brain, just as when we pull one end of a string the other end is moved, or when we push one end of a stick the other end is moved.[14]

In transmission, then, the little fibers in the nerves maintain their relative spatial

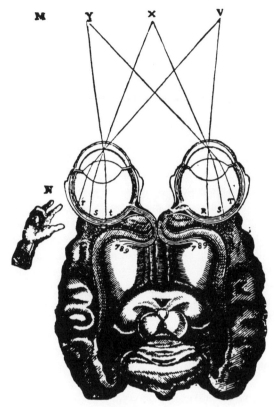

Figure 3.2

positions, so that the pattern of motions at the retina can be accurately reproduced in the cerebral cavities (i.e., by accurately preserving the topological relationships between all the points of the retinal image). Using the diagram pictured in figure 3.2, Descartes explains the point-to-point projection of the retinal image to the cerebral cavities. The motions light imparts to the optic nerves are transmitted in the following way: the rays that come from V touch at R the ends of the optic nerve coming from 7; so also the rays from X go from S to 8; and those from Y go to T and through the nerve to 9. Thus it is obvious, Descartes says, that another picture will form at 789 similar to objects V, X, and Y.

Vision, however, is not adequately explained by the mechanisms presented so far. Descartes believed it necessary that there be a further projection of the retinal images to the pineal gland and a merging of them to form one unified image.

Unification of Retinal Images at the Pineal Gland

REASONS FOR BELIEVING THAT THE RETINAL IMAGES ARE MERGED

At this point, a rather interesting similarity between Aristotle and Descartes emerges. It arises because both of them go beyond the physiological information available to them to postulate some sort of unification of the impressions from the senses on a physiological level, and they provide philosophical arguments for why this unification is necessary.

Aristotle hypothesizes that the channels from all the senses run to the heart[15] and that the impressions or movements from the senses are conveyed via the blood vessels, although there is controversy over whether he regards the "pneuma" or "vital air" that circulates with the blood as playing the main role in this transmission of impressions or whether it is the blood itself that does so.[16] That he had not actually traced the channels from all the senses is indicated by his argument in *De Juventute* that "because taste and touch can clearly be seen to extend to the heart, *hence the others also must lead to it*" (emphasis added).[17]

The key issue for understanding why Aristotle believes it necessary to postulate that the channels from all the senses run to the heart is his doctrine of the common sense. In the *De Anima*, he provides an argument that there must be a common sense faculty in order to account for our ability to discriminate between the objects of the special senses (e.g., white and sweet) (426b16–28). In the course of the argument, he notes that in order to do this it must be a unitary sense faculty that is able to perceive the objects of all the special senses (in this case vision and taste), but he does not identify any one organ as the seat of the common sense. Since the soul is the act or form of the body, it presumably relies for its ability to function upon the unity and interconnectedness of the body, but this does not necessarily imply even that the common sense or controlling sense faculty *has* an organ. If the common sense did have an organ, however, it would be necessary to transport the impressions from all of the senses to that organ.

In his more physiological works, however, Aristotle does appear to identify the heart as the primary locus of the sensitive soul (in the sense of being its source, spring, or "arche") and hence the primary locus also of the controlling sense faculty or common sense. At *De Juventute* 469a5–8, for example, he says the "source both of the sensitive and nutritive soul must be in the heart," and elsewhere he connects this with the fact that the heart is the origin and receptacle of the blood.[18] He also reasons that the heart develops before the brain and that the perceptual faculty must be present from the start since it distinguishes animals from plants (*DPA*, 666a33–36). And furthermore, the heart is in the middle of the body, and it is a single, uniform substance with an irregular shape. The oneness of the heart is of some importance since he believes that "the sensory soul is in all animals actually one; and this one-ness of the sensory soul determines a one-ness of the part in which it primarily abides" (*DPA*, 667b20–25).

If we do take the heart, then, as the primary locus of the sensitive soul and hence of the common sense, it is obviously necessary that the channels that convey impressions inward from all the senses converge there so that the common sense can perform its function of unifying these diverse inputs. And anything that prevented the impressions from reaching the heart would impede our perception.[19]

To what extent this sort of localization of the sensitive soul is compatible with Aristotle's view that the soul is the act or form of the animal as a whole is an important and troubling question but one that cannot be resolved here. What is of interest for our purposes is that Aristotle, like Descartes (at least in his physiological treatises), believes that there must be some sort of central sense organ to which all of the five senses are connected and that the controlling sense faculty or common sense is primarily located there. Both believe that the common sense accounts for the unity of our perceptual consciousness, although when Aristotle thinks about this he focuses primarily on the problem of how the inputs from the different senses are integrated together, rather than thinking, as Descartes does, about the problem of why we do not see double since an image is transmitted from each eye into the brain. Aristotle, in general, makes no attempt to explain the details of what occurs in the central organ or to account mechanically for the content of our perceptual consciousness as Descartes does.

Like those of Aristotle, Descartes' physiological hypotheses also go beyond what he actually had evidence for.[20] He did know that the optic nerves go to the cerebral cavities, although he knew very little about the details of the human visual system, since he dissected only animals himself. The diagram used in the *Dioptrics* (see fig. 3.2) is not drawn from a human brain but from that of a sheep.[21]

The second projection Descartes believes takes place in order to merge the two images at the pineal gland is entirely speculative from a physiological point of view. He admits in a letter to Mersenne in April 1640 that three years before, he had attended the autopsy of a woman and found himself unable even to recognize the pineal gland "even though I looked very thoroughly, and knew well where it should be, being accustomed to find it without any difficulty in freshly killed animals." The old professor performing the autopsy, he said, admitted that "he had never been able to see it in any human body."[22] It is, thus, for theoretical reasons that he postulated the merging of the retinal images and not because of any anatomical knowledge about the visual system.[23] In this, his procedure is the same as Aristotle's.

Descartes' main argument for believing that a merging of the two images must take place on a physiological level is that he believes it is necessary to account for the fact that we see one object although there are two retinal images conveyed inward to the brain. This line of reasoning is clearly put in a letter to Meysonnier in 1640: "Since we see only one thing with two eyes, and hear only one voice with two ears, and altogether have only one thought at a time, it must necessarily be the case that the impressions which enter by the two eyes or by the two ears, and so on unite with each other in some part of the body before being considered by the soul."[24]

Descartes' main reason for taking the pineal gland to be the place where this unification occurs is because "it is the only solid part in the brain which is single."[25] Or as he puts it in a letter to Mersenne, "Since the soul is not double, but single and indivisible, it seems to me that the part of the body to which it is most immediately joined should also be single."[26] And since all the other parts of the brain are bilaterally symmetrical, the soul must be joined immediately to the pineal gland.[27]

Both Descartes and Aristotle, then, believe that some sort of unification of the inputs or impressions from the senses must occur on a physiological level and that there must be a single organ in which this occurs.

THE MECHANICS OF THE TRANSMISSION TO THE PINEAL GLAND

Having selected the pineal gland as the seat of the soul, Descartes had to hypothesize that the optic nerves somehow connect to it (either directly or by means of the animal spirits). Since he knew that the nerves do not all connect to the pineal gland, he was forced to develop a complicated theory about the animal spirits having a connecting role. This could not be verified experimentally however, since he supposed that these spirits were too small to see and vanished with the death of the animal.

In the *Dioptrics*, Descartes says very little about the second projection of the images to the pineal gland, and no diagram is offered to illustrate it. After discussing the projection of the retinal image to the cerebral cavity, he says, "And from there I could again transport it right to a certain small gland . . . I could go even still further, to show you how sometimes it [the picture] can pass from there through the arteries of a pregnant woman, right to some specific member of the infant . . . and there forms these birthmarks."[28] Two things need to be noted here. First, the "picture" being transported is the retinal image considered as a pattern of motions—the motions being determined at each point by the ratio of spin to forward motion of the light particles. The relative positions of the points are preserved in transmission to the cerebral cavity as shown in the diagram (fig. 3.2) and are presumably also preserved in the transmission to the pineal gland. Second, such a "picture" seems hardly the sort of thing that could be transported through the blood, and Descartes makes no attempt to describe any plausible vehicle or mechanism for this taking place.

To make sense of this, I examine Descartes' more detailed account in *Treatise on Man*. This account goes part way towards reconciling the difficulty but not in a completely satisfactory manner. The element stressed in *Treatise on Man* is the role of the animal spirits. These are hardly mentioned in the *Dioptrics*, where only the motions in the nerve fibers transmitted to the pineal gland cause our sensations. In *Treatise on Man*, Descartes says the stimulation of certain nerve fibers causes the tubules of those nerves to dilate their openings in the cerebral cavities. This in turn causes the animal spirits flowing out of the pineal gland to flow more strongly toward those tubules and thus creates a sort of pattern traced on the pineal gland by the outflowing spirits. It is this pattern that is connected to our idea and not the pattern of motions in the nerve endings at the cerebral cavity.

This central role of the animal spirits is confirmed in a letter to Mersenne of 21 April 1641. Mersenne had objected to the pineal gland as the seat of the soul since no nerves connected to it. Descartes answered:

> It is impossible that they [the nerves] all connect to it otherwise than by means of the spirits, as they do at the pineal gland. It is certain also that the seat of the common sense must be very mobile, to receive the impressions which come from the senses; but it must be such that it can only be moved by the spirits which transmit these impressions, and only the pineal gland is of this sort.[29]

This, to some extent, helps to solve the problem of how the picture or image of the thing seen could be transmitted through the blood to the child in the womb, since the animal spirits form part of the blood. However, although it is easy to conceive of an image or pattern in the motions of the nerve endings in the cerebral cavity (or in the openness or closedness of the tubules, as Descartes stresses in *Treatise on Man*), or in the pattern traced on the pineal gland by the spirits leaving, it is difficult to understand how the spirits, which are in constant rapid movement, could convey an image through the arteries. But it is clear that Descartes thinks they do, because the same claim appears in *Treatise on Man*.[30] This sort of transmission of images by the spirits is also involved in his explanation of memory, which immediately follows the passage just quoted.

The most likely explanation for these theories being propounded by Descartes is that they are a carryover from the Aristotelian tradition, in which the cardiovascular system carries out many of the sensitive functions later assigned to the nervous system. Descartes does very little to integrate these earlier views with his own and seems to include them by force of habit without thinking out the mechanisms of the process very thoroughly.

Action of the Pineal Gland Image upon the Soul

The question, of course, that thrusts itself upon the philosopher who has followed the elaborate mechanisms all the way to the pineal gland is How does all this generate something as unlike it as our ideas or sensations? Descartes' answers on this point in the optical writings are rather crudely materialistic and disappointingly naive. In *Treatise on Man*, he says:

It is not those [figures] which are imprinted in the organs of external sense, or in the interior surface of the brain, but only those which are traced in the spirits on the surface of the gland H, where the seat of the imagination and common sense is located, which must be taken for ideas, that is to say for the forms or images which the reasonable soul considers immediately, when, united to this machine, she imagines or senses some object.

And a bit further on he says:

I want to include generally under the name "idea" all the impressions which the spirit can receive in flowing from the gland H, which are attributed to the common sense when they depend on the presence of objects, but they can also proceed from several other causes . . . and then it is to the imagination that they should be attributed.

And several paragraphs later he says, "After the spirits flowing from the gland H have there received the impression of some idea, they pass."[31] It is hard to avoid the interpretation that here we have the soul contemplating patterns traced by the spirits on the surface of the pineal gland and that these patterns are equated with ideas and said to be "what the soul considers immediately."

In the *Dioptrics* also, Descartes is able to do little more than assert that, strange as it may seem, these motions *do* act upon the soul to produce sensations: "It is the movements of which the picture is composed which, acting immediately on [*agissant contre*] our mind [*âme*] inasmuch as it is united to the body, are so established by nature to make it have such perceptions."[32] If pushed to explain this "nature," Descartes falls back on God, especially in later writings when his metaphysics has been better elaborated. God has affixed the various sensations to the motions. This is possible because the mind exists in quasi-substantial union with the body. If an angel were to be in a human body, it would perceive only the motions there, but not have sensations as we do.[33] What happens, then, in the human case is that what the soul is immediately considering is material in nature, but what we experience is a pattern of light and color (for vision), or thirst, pain, the smell of coffee, etc. In a sense, therefore, scholars such as Kemp Smith, Hamelin, and Reed are correct in saying that in perception what the mind contemplates or is immediately aware of are "ideas corporeas," or brain states.[34]

And furthermore, Descartes sometimes even speaks of the motions or images in our brains as "representing" objects to the soul.[35]

On a metaphysical level, the mind as subject confronts the patterns in the pineal gland as object. But we, unlike the hypothetical angel, do not experience a pattern of motions, but the sensations that God has joined to them, such as thirst, warmth, colors, etc.[36] Thus to say we are immediately aware of brain states, or indeed aware of them at all, is misleading.

What sensation we experience depends on which nerves are stimulated (those from the ears make us hear sounds, those from the tongue savors, etc.) and upon the good pleasure of God who connected various color sensations with particular sorts of motions in the brain. The mechanisms explained above, then, explain our perception of light and color: "We must think that our soul is of such a nature that the force of the movements which are found in the parts of the brain from which the optic nerves originate make it [the mind] have the sensation [*sentiment*] of light; and the manner [*façon*] of these movements that of color."[37]

The quantity of light that we see is determined by the force with which each of the optic nerves is moved, which is itself a function of a number of variables: the quantity of light in the objects,[38] their distance, the size of the pupil, and the amount of space that the rays from each part of the object occupy on the retina. Our vision of colors is likewise conditioned by these same physical variables. Specifically, we are able to perceive only as many differently colored parts of an object as there are optic nerve endings in that portion of the retina upon which its image is projected. The space occupied by the end of each of these nerves must be considered as a point. If an object has four thousand parts and there are only one thousand optic nerves in that portion of the retina, then each nerve would be moved in a kind of composite manner, and we would perceive only one thousand parts.[39] Thus distant fields or mountains appear to be all of one color. This account of visual color perception is, thus, the source of the view (held, for example, by Berkeley) that our visual field consists of a mosaic of unrelated visual points.

Color Perception and the Mechanisms of Vision

The above-described mechanisms would appear to provide what Descartes needed in his struggle against the scholastics—namely, a successful mechanistic account of our perception of one of the most important sensible qualities, color. More precisely, it accounts for our perception of a roughly two-dimensional color mosaic that replicates the retinal image. There is one important problem, however, with taking this theory to be an adequate account of light and color perception (apart, that is, from the problem of how motions can cause sensations). We do not, in fact, see things as they are represented in the retinal image. Even if the retinal image were transmitted to the pineal gland and the pattern of motions in the pineal gland acted upon the soul in such a way that our visual field was exactly the same as the retinal image (point for point), this mechanical transmission would fail to explain how such phenomena as size constancy and color constancy occur.

When we look at a familiar object, we do not see it change size even though the area it occupies on the retina changes radically as it approaches. But it would appear, on the basis of Descartes' theory, that we should. The problem of why we do not is what psychologists call the problem of size constancy. Colors, after all, are perceived (under normal conditions) as spread out in space and not as diffuse and all pervading like a scent; many colors appear at once and in various spatial relationships with each other. Thus, color perception and size and shape perception cannot be sharply separated.[40] And the fact that the relative areas objects occupy in our visual field are not the same as those they occupy in the retinal image has not been explained on the basis of Descartes' physiological theory.[41] Thus some supplementary mechanism or process must be invoked.

An even more troubling problem (not discussed by Descartes to my knowledge) is the problem of color constancy. Familiar objects under unusual lighting are frequently seen as having their normal colors. Thus, even the colors we see cannot be explained mechanically solely in terms of the motions of the light that hits the retina and the action of the nerves that transmit these motions to the pineal gland.[42]

The Significance of Descartes' Physiology

What stands out most clearly in Descartes' contributions to the physiology of vision is his attempt to explain our perception of a unified object based wholly upon anatomical structures and mechanically describable changes in the figure and/or motion of the retinae, nerves, animal spirits, pineal gland, and brain. He seems to think that he has explained our perception of the object if he has provided for the formation of a unified cerebral copy of it, or at least he believes such a copy is necessary. As I show in the next chapter, he realizes that some supplementary mechanisms are required, but the material presented above still provides the essential core of his theory of vision. His theory thus provides a kind of mechanized Aristotelianism. While Aristotelians speak of the *form* of the object being received by the senses, Descartes develops a theory in which the *figure* traced by the object on the retina is transmitted to the pineal gland (where it acts upon the soul).[43]

Unfortunately, this zeal to provide a unified cerebral image of the object led Descartes into unfounded and erroneous physiological speculations as well as on a more subtle level, leading him to wrongly see the eye as functioning like a camera. Although the basic idea of a point-to-point projection of retinal images to the brain has stood the test of time, the hypothesis that they are merged to form one image has not. Retinal images are projected into several different areas of the brain and are subject to considerable topological distortion, and although the nerves from corresponding retinal points in the two eyes have been traced to contiguous brain areas, there is no evidence that they are ever actually merged.[44] Thus the unity of our perceptual experience cannot be accounted for by physiology alone. Modern science thus destroys the physiological basis for any very straightforward copy theory of perception. Descartes' physiological theory, by contrast, sets us up for this sort of theory.[45]

Descartes' account of the basic physiology and functioning of the visual system had considerable influence upon subsequent philosophers, such as Malebranche, Locke, and Berkeley.[46] Even when they disagree with certain aspects of his theory,[47] they continue to accept Descartes' account of the basic mechanics of vision—the function of the lens, retina, optic nerves, the point-to-point projection of the retinal image to the brain, etc. As a result, they face many of the same problems, especially since they, like Descartes (and perhaps even more than Descartes), tend to think of perception in terms of visual perception. This does not, of course, result in total uniformity in the way they resolve the problems. Different philosophers within the Cartesian tradition have different ideas—for example, about the nature of colors as they exist in objects, or whether they exist in objects at all, or on where to draw the line between seeing and judging in perception. But these problems are posed and answered within the framework set out by Descartes.

I turn in the final chapter to the problem of visual spatial perception and to the question of how our perception of situation, distance, size, and shape differs from our perception of color.

4

Descartes' Theory of
Visual Spatial Perception

WE TURN, IN THIS FINAL CHAPTER, TO WHAT IS PERHAPS THE MOST INTEREST-
ing and certainly the most controversial part of Descartes' theory of vision—
namely, visual spatial perception. Included under spatial perception are our
perception of situation and distance, as well as our perception of size and shape
(since our perception of these is interconnected with our perception of situation
and distance). Since properties like size and shape are essential to Descartes'
physics, scholars have very naturally been interested in the questions of whether
we can discover the sizes and shapes of objects through sense perception, how
we do so, and what degree of certainty can be attached to such perceptions.[1]

Aristotle, interestingly, says nothing about our perception of situation and
distance and not very much about our perception of size and shape. Since size
and shape are common sensibles, their perception would be the province of the
common sense, which would perceive them through the proper sensibles (see
chap. 1), but his account of light and color did not go very far towards explaining
how vision supplies the necessary information for making discriminations of size
and shape.[2] The problem was that Aristotle failed to explain why, if colored
bodies produce qualitative changes in all parts of the medium to which they have
rectilinear access, the eye is not affected by them all at once, resulting in
complete confusion. The work of Alhazen was designed to fill this gap, and the
perspectivists built upon his work, integrating it with Aristotelian and Neoplatonic
elements. Their theory of light (discussed briefly in chap. 2) taken together with
Kepler's account of the formation of the retinal image, which grew out of the
perspectivist tradition (discussed in chap. 3), provided a coherent account of what
happened between the object and the retina on which Descartes could build in
order to explain spatial perception.[3]

Descartes' physiology, in a way, simply extends the same sort of analysis
Kepler had provided one step further. Kepler had explained how the rays from
each point on the object were reunited at a corresponding point on the retina;
Descartes establishes a similar point-to-point correspondence between the retinal
image and the pineal gland image. But his commitment to this theory makes

visual spatial perception particularly problematic for him. As noted in chapter 3, there are some problems even with Descartes' claim that he had provided a fully adequate mechanistic account of color perception. But his mechanistic account is even more inadequate for explaining our visual perception of situation, distance, size, and shape than it is for explaining color perception. Some sort of supplementary mechanisms in addition to the point-to-point projection of the retinal images to the brain and their merging at the pineal gland must be postulated. But of what sort? Is it merely that the mechanisms involved are more complex, or must we have recourse to a different sort of model altogether? In his scientific writings on vision, Descartes attempts to explain as much as he can mechanistically, but he postulates corrective judgments by the mind in some cases where he finds himself unable to provide a mechanistic explanation. He thus employs two different models.

When employing the mechanistic model, Descartes explains our perceptual abilities by reference to the way motions are transmitted to our brains from objects (changes in eye shape, for example, cause changes in that part of our brains from which the nerves going to the eye muscles originate). The last stage in the process—namely, our conscious experience—occurs simply as a result of the way in which the complex patterns of motions in our brains have been connected with sensations by God; the mind itself is passive in its reception of them and does not make any judgments or perform any sort of calculations.

When he comes to explain visual spatial perception, however, Descartes is increasingly driven to have recourse to another quite different model—the homunculus model. This model involves an inner judge and is based on the supposition that certain perceptual abilities (such as monocular distance perception) require actual reasoning and judgment on the part of the mind (regarded as a sort of inner judge). When using the homunculus model, Descartes must distinguish between the judgments the mind makes and the data on the basis of which it makes them. It is clear that the retinal image and its pineal correlate have a special status here, but unclear just what that status is.

Descartes' thinking about which model to employ is still in flux in the optical writings, and as a result, the distinction between what we perceive by sense and what involves judgment by the mind is not sharply drawn. For example, in his account of shape perception in *Treatise on Man*, Descartes does not include a reference to any sort of judgment or reasoning because he thinks it is explainable merely by the fact that a resembling shape is traced on the retina, but in the *Dioptrics*, he clearly specifies that our knowledge of figure is judgmental. Descartes is generally ambivalent about the role of judgment in the *Dioptrics* also. Perceiving the situation of objects by sight is not said to involve judgment,[4] although it *may* involve the mind directing its attention out from points on the retina. (The ability to do this is something the mind has because it is united with the body and is therefore aware of the relative spatial locations of the parts of the body). At least one of the means for perceiving distance—namely, eye shape— seems to involve no judgment or reasoning by the mind, and even the famous natural geometry theory, at least for the case of binocular vision, could be read in such a way as not to involve judgment. Descartes is driven most clearly to employ the homunculus model and to unequivocally postulate an act of judgment in the case of size and shape perception.

In the Sixth Replies, Descartes moves in the direction of the homunculus model by emphasizing the role of judgment in visual perception. In spite of his claim that he is only reiterating what he says in the *Dioptrics,* the differences between the two accounts are significant. I begin by considering carefully his position as explained in the *Dioptrics,* since his remarks on vision in subsequent works do not constitute a complete or coherent theory by themselves. After my examination of the *Dioptrics,* I briefly summarize my findings about the distinction between seeing and judging in those texts and point to some unresolved problems with Descartes' theory there.

I conclude by examining Descartes' account of perception in the Sixth Replies and compare it with the one articulated in his earlier scientific writings on vision. I argue that this account differs from the earlier one, suffers from serious internal problems, and not only fails to resolve the problems left outstanding in the optical writings, it exacerbates them.

Visual Spatial Perception in the Optical Writings

SITUATION

The most basic element of our visual spatial perception is our perception of the situation of objects—which Descartes defines as the direction they lie in relative to our body (what psychologists call "egocentric spatial perception"). This is a problem because the retinal image is inverted (up-down) and reversed (right-left), so that it would seem that we should be misled about the locations of objects. It is also a problem because in perception, the soul is in direct contact only with the pattern of motions traced by the departing animal spirits at the surface of the pineal gland, and thus it is something of a mystery how the soul can perceive an object as out from us in space at all.

It would seem that the first problem could be resolved mechanically simply by reinverting the image between the cerebral cavities and the pineal gland. In fact, this has sometimes been thought to be Descartes' own solution[5] based on a drawing given in *Treatise on Man* that shows a reinversion (fig. 4.1). However, the figure is not referred to in the section where he discusses situation perception and was not Descartes' own drawing, having been added by someone else after

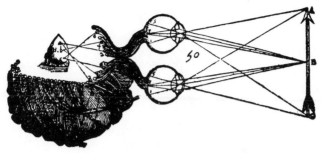

Figure 4.1

his death.[6] And a little reflection shows why this does not solve the problem of situation perception. If the situation of an object is the direction it lies in *relative to my body*,[7] then my perception of the spatiality of my own body must be an essential element in that perception; the presence of either a right-side-up or an upside-down image in the pineal gland does not solve the problem for, considered alone, it tells us nothing about the spatial location of what is represented in the image relative to my body. Descartes thus falls back, and relies very heavily, on our perception of the spatiality of our own body—which enables him also to provide a sort of solution to the second problem of how we perceive objects as out from us in space.

> We do not perceive it [situation] otherwise by means of our eyes, than we do by means of our hands; and our knowledge of it does not depend on any image, or on any action which comes from the object, but only on the position of the little parts of the brain, from which the nerves take their origin; for this position, changing however slightly each time the position of the parts of the body where these nerves are inserted changes, is instituted by nature so that the soul can know not only where each part of the body it animates is relative to the other parts, but also so that the soul can transfer its attention from each part to all the places on the straight lines which one can imagine stretched from the extremity of each of these parts to infinity.[8]

Our knowledge of the spatial position of our own body (something that we possess by an "institution of nature"—i.e., God simply connected our mind with our body in this way) is thus the necessary basis for our perception of the spatial location of physical objects. Descartes then goes on to develop an explanation of situation perception in which vision is treated as, essentially, a form of touch. Our eyes do not touch objects, obviously, so Descartes is forced to use the analogy between vision and a blind man with a stick—the light rays playing the role of the stick. To explain situation perception, he develops this analogy on two different levels. The simpler solution to the situation perception problem involves our awareness of the direction in which our eye or head is turned and

Figure 4.2

is analogous to the blind man's awareness of the direction in which his hands are turned. This is the only solution given in *Treatise on Man* where Descartes merely says that we know the situation of objects because of the changes in the muscles or nerves accompanying the turning of the eyes to look at different objects.[9]

But not all situation perception depends upon these mechanisms, for we are able to perceive the relative situations of several objects at once (i.e., seen with one eye fixation), and eye or head movements are of no use here. In order to explain this, Descartes adapts the blind man with crossed sticks analogy to the case by taking two different points on the retina to be analogous with the blind man's two hands. He develops this as follows:

> If he turns his hands A and C toward E [see fig. 4.2], the nerves inserted in the hand cause a certain change in his brain which gives his soul the means of knowing not only the places A and C, but also all the others which are on the straight lines AE or CE, so that the soul can direct its attention as far as objects B and D, and determine the places where they are, without for this purpose having to know or think in any way about the places where his two hands are.
>
> Now, if our eye or our head turns in some direction, our soul is informed of this by the changes which the nerves, inserted in the muscles used in these movements, cause in our brain. As here, in the eye RST we must think that the position of the optic nerve which is at point R, S or T [see fig. 3.2, p. 57], is followed by another

certain position of the part of the brain 7, 8 or 9 which enables the soul to know the places which are on the line RV, or SX or TY: so that you must not find it strange that objects can be seen in their true situation although the picture which they print in the eye has a wholly contrary situation. Thus, our blind man can sense the object B which is to the right by means of his left hand, and D which is to the left by means of his right hand.[10] (Translation mine)

Although mention is made of our turning our eyes or head (the first mechanism mentioned), Descartes seems to be suggesting also that seeing object Y to the left by means of our optic nerve T to the right is to be understood as like the blind man feeling object B to the left by means of hand C to the right. And since the blind man directs his attention out from his hands in straight lines (along the lines made by his sticks), it would seem in this case also that some sort of directing of attention out from points on our retina along straight lines (this time light rays) is implied.

This passage is the source from which later optical writers take their solution to the problem of situation perception. But whereas in this passage no explicit mention is made of the mind tracing back along light rays (as Berkeley describes it),[11] this is how the solution was understood by later writers. And certainly Descartes implies that some sort of directing of attention is involved, and along straight lines would be the path light rays would follow.

The account given here, however, is difficult to interpret. On the one hand, Descartes says that the blind man knows the places A and C where his hands are and directs his attention out from them toward the object, and on the other hand, he says that he does not have to know or think in any way about the places where his two hands are. Which of these we settle on makes a difference, for if the blind man knows the relative positions of his hands and directs his attention out from those places on straight lines, then in the analogous case of vision, the "tracing back along the rays" interpretation would be in the spirit of Descartes' explanation. On the other hand, if he really does not know or think in any way about where his hands are, then it is not; certain motions conveyed to our brains simply cause our perceptions of the situation of objects. The first interpretation is cast in terms of the homunculus model, while the second is cast in terms of the mechanical model. (The details of how this could be worked out on the mechanical model constitute the problem psychologists call "directional sensitivity of the retina.")

Had Descartes stuck to the mechanical model, his only explanation of why we perceive objects as out from us in space rather than in our eyes or hands, or in our brains (since that is where the motions are), would have to be that God simply chose to annex our perceptual awareness of the situation of objects external to us in space to certain motions in our brain because this would be conducive to the preservation and well-being of the soul-body composite. Apparently he found this sort of explanation insufficient, perhaps because of its failure to include any reference to our perception of the spatiality of our own bodies, and hence, he introduced the soul's ability to transfer its attention out from various body parts to ascertain the situation of objects relative to the body.

One difficulty with Descartes' explanation is that the analogy between sight and a rather specialized case of tactual perception (the blind man with a stick) is a rather weak analogy. For while a blind man *can* think about where his hands are and direct his attention out from them in straight lines, we cannot think about the relative positions of points on our retinae or direct our attention out from them in straight lines, since we are never conscious of the spatial position of our retinae or points on them. Furthermore, directing our attention is a mental act, and since Descartes equates mind with consciousness, a mental act of which we cannot be aware (such as directing our attention out from different points on our retinae) would be impossible in principle.

It should also be noted here that here the extent that Descartes' account of situation perception relies on the soul's ability to be present in the hands or eyes and to direct its attention out from them in straight lines, it is in tension with his position in the preceding discourse. In the fourth discourse of the *Dioptrics* he states that the soul senses inasmuch as it is present in the brain where it exercises the faculty of the common sense and that while remaining in the brain it can, by means of the nerves, receive impressions from external objects.[12] How, then, can it be present in the hands or eyes? Perhaps the apparent inconsistency could be reconciled along the lines of Descartes' explanation in a letter to Mersenne that the soul can "utilize" other body parts but is "immediately joined" only to the pineal gland.[13] The notion of the soul using the body, however, harks back to the older Platonic form of dualism in which the soul is radically non-spatial and therefore does not fit well with Descartes' form of dualism, in which the soul is localized at the pineal gland.

DISTANCE

Descartes builds his account of visual distance perception on his explanation of situation perception; it involves the question of how far away the object is rather than simply the direction in which it lies. Since the retinal image is two-dimensional, some supplementary mechanisms are obviously needed. Descartes provides five means by which distance is perceived or seen, two of which involve the controversial "natural geometry" theory. His discussion of distance perception was very influential on subsequent writers, such as Malebranche and Berkeley. By contrast with Malebranche and Berkeley, Descartes' explanation of distance perception is noteworthy in that (1) he does not deal explicitly with the problem of our perception of externality (why do we perceive objects as external at all) that so troubled Malebranche and Berkeley; (2) he does not draw a sharp distinction between seeing and judging but instead is rather careless and inconsistent in his use of terminology, speaking of distance alternately as "perceived" (*aperçevoir*), "seen" (*voir*), "judged" (*juger*), or simply as "known" (both *connaître* and *savoir* are used); and (3) some of the things he lists as means of perceiving distance are things we are not (and probably could not be) conscious of, whereas Malebranche and Berkeley admit only means of which we can be aware.

Eye Shape

The first non-geometrical explanation for our ability to perceive distance visually involves the shape of the eye. This shape must be different for us to see nearby objects clearly than it is when we perceive distant objects. This we know from the experiment described earlier with the dissected eye: the shape of the eye must change (or be changed by pressure) in order for objects at different distances to be brought into focus on the retina. Thus, Descartes supposes that in normal vision, we change the shape of our eye in order to enable us to proportion it to the distance of the objects, and this moves parts of our brain in a way instituted by nature to make our soul perceive this distance: "And this happens to us ordinarily without our having to reflect about it; in the same way as when we grasp some object with our hand we make it conform to the size and shape of the object, and feel it by this means, without for this having to think about these movements."[14]

This explanation is clearly cast in terms of the mechanical model. Eye shape varies regularly with distance, and thus it can cause changes in our brain that vary regularly with distance. These changes in the position or motion of parts of our brain cause our perceptions of differing distances because of the way God connected our soul and our body. There is no need for the perceiver to be aware of the shape of his eye as such, although Descartes does not actually deny that we are or that we can be aware of it.

The next two means for perceiving distance Descartes describes involve the controversial "natural geometry" theory on which Berkeley centered his attack in the *New Theory of Vision*. The theory is expounded in the *Dioptrics* first in terms of binocular vision and then for monocular vision, although the account in *Treatise on Man* includes only the binocular.

In speaking of natural geometry, Descartes, of course, has Euclidean geometry in mind. In the wake of Berkeley's sharp bifurcation between visible and tangible objects, the question has been raised whether visual space is Euclidean, and many people have argued that it is not Euclidean, but that it conforms to some kind of elliptical geometry (although they concede that the space we experience through touch is Euclidean).[15] This issue can be bypassed, however, for purposes of understanding Descartes' natural geometry theory, since Descartes invokes geometry only to explain the way we perceive how far away objects are from us and not the geometrical properties of the objects seen. Also his analysis assimilates vision to touch as much as possible, and it is conceded that the space we experience by touch is Euclidean.

Natural Geometry

Binocular distance perception. The first of the geometrical means for telling how far away objects are relies on the fact that we have two eyes that are separated from each other and that can be turned in such a way that they look at the same object. Since this theory involves knowledge of the direction our eyes are turned in, it builds on the way in which Descartes explains our ability to know this in his discussion of situation perception. We "know" distance, he says (and here the French verb is *connaître*, which has the meaning of "to be acquainted with"— the same verb he uses in the situation section),

> by the relation which the two eyes have to each other. For as our blind man, holding two sticks AE, CE, whose length I suppose him not to know, and knowing [*savoir*] only the distance between his two hands A and C, and the size of the angles ACE and CAE, can from that, as though by a natural geometry, know [*connaître*] where E is; thus when our two eyes RST and rst are turned toward X, the length of the line SS and size of the two angle XSs and XsS make us know [*connaître*] where the point X is.[16] (See figs. 4.2 and 3.2.)

There are several interesting things about this passage. The first is his use of the verbs *savoir* and *connaître*. The verb *savoir* (connoting an intellectual kind of knowledge) is used to describe the blind man's knowledge of the distance between his hands and the angles made by the sticks, while *connaître* (meaning "to be acquainted with") is used to describe his knowledge of where the point E is. In the parallel passage in *Treatise on Man* Descartes uses the two verbs in exactly the same way.[17] He seems to be trying through this use of the different verbs to arrive at the sort of directness and immediacy associated with the verb *connaître*, starting from intellectual and perhaps implicitly mathematical knowledge.

Another interesting thing about this passage is that Descartes' reference to natural geometry occurs in his discussion of the blind man, whereas in the case of vision, he says that the length of the line and the size of the angles "make us know" (*connaître*) where the point E is. He does the same thing in the situation section where he talks about the soul transferring its attention out from the hands along straight lines, but then he says in the case of vision that the changes in the brain caused by our turning our eyes "make us know" the places along the straight lines. Although this difference may be insignificant, since Descartes wants us to think of the case of vision as like that of the blind man, still I think Descartes is responding to a significant difference between the cases. The blind man can deliberately think about where his hands are, how far apart they are, the direction his hands are turned, and the angles the sticks make, but it is not clear that we can do this with our eyes for vision. In the case of the blind man, then, he employs the homunculus model—speaking of the transferring of attention, the use of natural geometry, etc. But in the case of vision, he is still thinking of providing a purely mechanistic account similar to the one he provides for eye shape. Certain changes in our muscles and brain simply cause us to know the distance or situation of objects because God chose to conjoin these movements with our perception of them.

One last thing to be noted is that, in this passage, Descartes says that we know where the point E is "as though by a natural geometry" and does not claim that we actually *use* geometry—a claim that would indeed cause all sorts of problems even in the more plausible blind man case. It may be plausible to assert that the blind man knows the direction his hands are turned, but surely one would hesitate, for example, to say that he knows his hands are eighteen inches apart and that the base angles formed by the sticks are fifty-five degrees. This would obviously be a hopeless over-intellectualization of perception.

Monocular distance perception. The above means for perceiving distance would be useless for monocular distance perception; a blind man with only one stick, the length of which he does not know, could not determine with one poke of the stick how far away an object is. Thus, Descartes reasons, a person with only one eye must look at the object from point S and then move to look at it with the same eye from point s (see fig. 3.2).

> This will suffice to make the size of the line Ss and of the two angles XSs and XsS found together in our imagination, and to make us notice the distance of point X; and this by an act of thought which, being only a completely simple imagination, nonetheless includes within itself a reasoning similar to that which surveyors use when they measure inaccessible places by means of two different observation points.[18]

Here, at last, we have an explicit reference to an "act of reasoning." However, its status is quite unclear. It is an act of thought essentially involving the imagination, since the imagination retains the information necessary for determining the distance of the object—namely, the length of the line and the size of the angles. It is a simple act of thought, presumably because we discover no parts in it; it occurs in such a way that we are not aware of making any inferences or doing any reasoning. Yet it includes an act of reasoning. Why, one might ask, does Descartes find it necessary to postulate an act of reasoning here?

There are several possible reasons. The most distinctive thing about this case is that it necessarily involves memory, at least the sort of short-term memory involved in the imagination retaining information between the first and second eye fixations. This, however, seems to be merely the sort of corporeal memory we share with the animals and not anything that would make it necessary to postulate an act of reasoning.

Another possible reason is because we find with both binocular and monocular distance perception a certain sort of irreducible complexity not found with our perception of situation. Given Descartes' explanation of vision by means of a point-by-point projection of the retinal image to the pineal gland, one fixation of one eye just cannot be enough—either two eyes or two eye fixations are required. Thus, it would seem that the mind must somehow be involved in the comparing and combining of the different inputs. This may well be what moves Descartes to speak of reasoning here, although if it is, it is not clear that the necessity of combining several inputs requires us to postulate any reasoning process or involvement of the mind. After all, several inputs are involved in even the simplest of perceptions—such as my seeing a blue object to my right, which involves at minimum the different motions that cause me to perceive blue plus the changes in the brain that enable me to tell which direction my eyes and head are turned. There seems, thus, in principle, no reason why a mechanistic explanation could not accomodate any number of inputs simply by hypothesizing that when all these changes occur in the brain simultaneously, they cause us to have certain perceptions, without reference to the mind needing to go through any reasoning process.

The only other possible reason for postulating an act of reasoning here is that in these two cases the inputs to be combined are at least implicitly mathematical— the length of lines and the size of angles—so it would seem that the powers of reason would be required. An animal would, presumably, be quite incapable of perceiving distance in this way. Had Descartes provided any account of animals' visual spatial perception, it would have been very helpful for our understanding of human distance perception, but the part of the *Principles* that was to deal with plants and animals was never completed.

Broader Significance of the Natural Geometry Theory

Several subsequent writers have attributed great philosophical importance to the natural geometry theory presented in the *Dioptrics*. Berkeley, coming on the scene at a time when the view that we immediately or directly perceive only ideas was prevalent, saw the natural geometry theory as providing a necessary and an a priori means for telling how far away objects are and believed that if this were true, the existence of objects out from us in space would be established (and his immaterialism thus disproved).[19] There is no evidence, however, that Descartes viewed the natural geometry theory as having any such important epistemological role or even that he perceived at the time of writing the *Dioptrics* the seriousness of the problem of externality perception. Hints of such an awareness appear in the Sixth Replies, where Descartes attributes our perception of the external existence of the stick to an act of judgment. But in the *Dioptrics* and *Treatise on Man* he does not even raise this issue. Our means for knowing distance are, as he stresses in both works, highly approximate and fallible.[20] But he expresses no doubt that there are objects external to us and that we perceive them as such.

Nancy Maull's very interesting argument that the purpose of the natural geometry theory is to establish the applicability of Euclidian geometry to nature (Kant's problem) is open to the same objections. Whether or not the natural geometry theory can be seen by hindsight to fill this gap in Descartes' philosophical system, Maull clearly goes beyond the evidence in supposing that this is Descartes' intention in developing it.[21] Maull suggests that Descartes imported geometrical reasoning into his psychophysiological theory of perception quite intentionally to answer the questions: (1) How is a priori geometry (specifically three-dimensional Euclidean geometry) applicable to nature? and (2) How is mathematical science of nature possible? To establish this claim, she would have to show from the texts that Descartes was aware of the gap she points to—namely, the need to prove somehow that geometry is applicable to nature—and that he saw the natural geometry theory as doing this. This she does not do, and in the absence of such evidence, I believe we should be wary of overreading the text. Indeed, the brevity of Descartes' presentation of the natural geometry theory (twenty-three lines total for both binocular and monocular distance perception) weigh against his having had such grandiose purposes for it as either Berkeley or Maull suggest.

Confusion/Distinctness and Force of Light

To illustrate this second non-geometrical means for perceiving distance, Descartes has recourse to the illustration he uses earlier to illustrate retinal image formation, complete with the dark room and the man inside looking at the back of the dissected eye. We can, he says, use the confusion or distinctness of the shape (of the object seen) and force or weaknesss of the light coming from them to see how far away they are (see fig. 3.1).

As when we fix our eyes on X, the rays which come from objects 10 and 12 are not reunited as exactly at R and T on our retina as they would be if the objects were at points V and Y; from which we see that they are farther away from us or closer to us than X is. Then from the fact that the light which comes from object 10 towards our eye is stronger than if the object were toward V, we judge it to be closer, and from the fact that the light which comes from object 12 is feebler than if it came from toward Y, we judge it farther away.[22]

Descartes' definition of confusion and distinctness here is clearly given in optical terms. The image of an object projected on our retina is distinct when the light rays from each point on the object are accurately reunited by the lens at a corresponding point on the retina and confused when this is not the case. There is, however, an unexplained gap between a statement about how accurately the rays from each point of an object are reunited at a corresponding retinal point and a statement such as "from which we see that they are farther away from us or closer to us than X is."

If we were simply to consider this passage with its accompanying diagram in isolation, the most natural reading would be to suppose that the soul, like the man in the dark room, gazes upon the retinal image and determines certain things about the objects from it. (This would be the most extreme form of the homunculus model.) We know, however, that this cannot be what Descartes means here, both because the soul exercises its sensory functions at the pineal gland (not the retina) and because he clearly realizes that the soul has no eyes.[23]

How, then, can Descartes say that from the confusion of the image of an object on our retina, we can see that it is farther away from or closer to us than the point on which our eye is focused?

He does seem to be thinking in terms of the homunculus model rather than the mechanical model. The force or weakness of the light *could*, perhaps, be connected in a purely mechanical way with our perception of distance, much as eye shape is, but Descartes does not seem to want to make this move, since he postulates a judgment based on the strength or weakness of the light. Confusion and distinctness, however, seem to be in a different category. They are defined relationally in terms of the causal origin of light rays at particular points on the object and are impossible to specify in purely mechanical terms. No pattern of figure and motion is intrinsically distinct but is so only in relation to the object whose "image" it is.

If, however, the soul is reasoning from confusion or distinctness to distance, what confusion or distinctness in particular is it reasoning from? The retinal image itself is ruled out by the considerations cited above. The pattern of motions in the pineal gland seems an unlikely candidate, since it is hard to see how such a pattern of motions could be confused or distinct in the way an optical image can. Perhaps Descartes is supposing that our immediate visual experience is identical with the retinal image, so that every feature of the image is found in the experience. This is the most plausible interpretation, although it is subject to the objection that we do not, after all, see the sizes or shapes of objects as they are presented in the retinal image, so that therefore our immediate visual experience does not correspond exactly to the retinal image.

Previous Knowledge or Opinion

The last means Descartes gives by which we are enabled to perceive the distance of an object is that if we

> already imagine from someplace else the size of an object, or its situation, or the distinctness of its shape and of its colors, or merely the force of the light that comes from it, this can enable us, not properly to see, but to imagine its distance. For example when we observe from afar some body we are used to seeing close at hand, we judge its distance much better than we would if its size were not so well known to us.[24]

If we look at a sunlit mountain beyond a shaded forest, we know the forest is closer only by its situation. And if we see two boats on the sea that look of equal size (the smaller one being proportionately closer), we are able to judge which of them is closer by the differences in their shapes, colors, and the force of the light.

This group of "means" by which we are enabled to perceive the distance of objects functions as a sort of catchall category. It includes cases that involve prior knowledge, such as our knowledge of the normal size of boats with certain shapes enabling us to tell which is closer. Here Descartes explicitly denies that we *see* its distance, presumably because an aborigine who had never seen boats could not make use of this particular means of perceiving distance. He does not appear, however, to intend to limit this means only to cases where an opinion acquired by prior learning is involved. The situation of the forest relative to the mountain is perceived at the same time as we perceive the force of the light coming to us from them, and Descartes makes no mention of our previous knowledge about the size of the mountain. If we read him this way, then the door is opened to a virtually unlimited interaction between our perception of distance and our perception of all the other qualities of objects and thus to a potentially greatly expanded role for complicated reasoning and judgments by the mind—a line of thought that Descartes develops further in the Sixth Replies.

SIZE AND SHAPE

Descartes' account of size and shape perception is of considerable philosophical interest both because of the difference in the treatment of shape betweeen *Treatise on Man* and the *Dioptrics* and because the account of both given in the *Dioptrics* provides us with perhaps the clearest example of Descartes' use of the homunculus model for explaining perception.

In *Treatise on Man*, Descartes says that the soul can know the shape of an

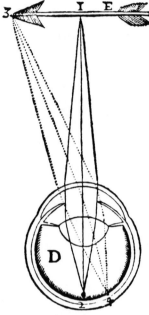

Figure 4.3

object: "She [the soul] can know the shape of an object inasmuch as the rays from point I come together at point 2 against the optic nerve, and those from point 3 at point 4, and so on, there tracing one [figure] which corresponds exactly to [*se rapporter à*] its own [the object]" (see fig. 4.3).[25] This seems fairly straightforward. We perceive the shape of an object because it is traced upon our retina and transmitted to the pineal gland. However, by the time Descartes wrote the *Dioptrics,* he saw the process as far more complicated. He writes, "Figure is judged by the knowledge or opinion we have of the situation of the different parts of the object, and not by the resemblance of the pictures in the eye: for these pictures usually contain only ovals and rhombuses when they make us see circles and squares."[26] Thus, although figure perception appears to be explainable by the same mechanisms that account for light and color perception—namely, the point-by-point projection of the retinal image to the brain and pineal gland—Descartes came to realize that perspective distortions must be corrected for.

Parallel passages on size can be compared in the two texts. In *Treatise on Man,* he states that "the soul can know the size of the objects of sight and all other similar qualities, simply by the knowledge which it has of the distance and situation of all their points; as also reciprocally, it judges sometimes of their distance by the opinion it has of their size."[27] And in the *Dioptrics,* he says:

Their size is estimated by the knowledge or opinion we have of their distance, compared with the size of the images which they imprint on the bottom of the eye; and not absolutely by the size of these images, as is obvious enough from the fact that when they [the images] are a hundred times larger when the objects are very close to us, they do not, for all that, make us see them as 100 times larger, but as nearly the same size, at least if we are not deceived about their distance.[28]

While in *Treatise on Man* Descartes says that distance perception and size perception are interconnected and involve judgment, the account in the *Dioptrics* specifies that the sizes of the images in the bottom of the eye are one of the inputs that go into the formation of that judgment. Speaking in this way, however, exposes him to the same very serious problems about the status of the retinal image already noted in the discussion of confusion and distinctness, without coming any closer to resolving them here than he did before.

Dioptrics: Concluding Remarks

SEEING AND JUDGING IN THE DIOPTRICS

Descartes in his optical writings does not articulate a sharp distinction between pure sensation on the one hand and judgments by the mind on the other. Instead, his accounts of how we perceive light, color, situatuion, distance, size, and shape are arranged on a kind of continuum ranging from purely anatomical and physiological factors at one end, which cause our sensations as a result of the way God conjoined our minds and bodies, to a variety of rather ill-defined mental processes at the other. Our perception of a unified object can be explained entirely by anatomical mechanisms. Our perception of light and color is close to the physiological/anatomical end of the spectrum and so also are distance perception based on the shape of the eye and at least simple kinds of situation perception, such as seeing that a bird is to my right by means of my awareness of turning my head to my right.[29] Size and shape perception and distance perception based on previous knowledge or opinion are at the other end. Monocular distance perception is similar to size and shape in its reliance on reasoning by the mind, but this is less clearly true of binocular distance perception, which is therefore closer to the anatomical/physiological end of the spectrum than monocular perception. But the sort of sharp dichotomy between seeing and judging found in, say, Berkeley, or even in Descartes' own later writing such as his Sixth Replies is not yet present. Questions about exactly where sense ends and reasoning begins, thus, have no clear answer.

One reason for this is the involvement of the spatiality of our own body in situation and distance perception. Changes occur in the brain that enable us to know the relative spatial locations of parts of our body and to direct our attention out from these in straight lines. We do not simply have motions in our brain to go on, as it were, since God has conjoined our minds and bodies in such a way that these motions give us an awareness of the position of various parts of our bodies. This is an institution of nature; we do not need to retrace the nerves to our extremities or engage in any sort of geometrical calculations—the awareness is simply given to us. And it forms the foundation of our ability to know the direction in which objects lie relative to our body. Since situation perception is a component of the mechanisms described as natural geometry, this enables Descartes to assimilate vision to touch in a way that downplays the explicitly mathematical elements in his account of distance perception.

Another possible reason for Descartes not drawing a sharp distinction between seeing and judging might be that drawing this distinction is not particularly central to his own purposes in the optical writings. So long as he is able to explain vision without recourse to the scholastic conceptual apparatus and to make suggestions for the improvement of vision based on his theory, he regards his theory as successful. And if he finds it necessary to draw the distinction between seeing and judging differently in some other context (as he does in his Sixth Replies), he believes he can do so without thereby radically altering his basic theory of vision in the *Dioptrics*.

UNRESOLVED PROBLEMS

One issue requiring further explanation is the relationship between the mechanical model and the homunculus model. While Descartes may be entitled to use two different models, he appears unaware that he is doing so and therefore fails to address some important questions. How are we to tell when we should employ one model rather than the other? Are some types of perceptual abilities wholly explainable by only one of the models or are both of them operative in all perception? If both are operative, how can the soul be, at the same time, wholly passive (as it is on the mechanical model) and actively involved in reasoning and judging (as it is on the homunculus model)? Is there any reason, in principle, why we must retain the homunculus model, or could it be dispensed with as our mechanistic explanations become increasingly sophisticated?

A related problem is the status of such judgments as those by which we perceive the correct size or shape of objects in spite of the facts that they take up far more space in the retinal image when they are close than when they are far away and that their images are subject to perspective distortions. These are anomalous for two reasons: first, because it is clear that the retinal image and/or its pineal correlate have a privileged status in vision but very unclear what that status is. Descartes clearly rejects the view that the soul somehow gazes at the retinal image on the grounds that it would require the soul to have eyes. Yet his account of size perception, for example, requires that we have access to the retinal image in *some* sense. In what sense do we and in what sense do we not have access to it? Second, given Descartes' dualistic metaphysics, any judgment (being mental) must be something we are aware of or at least *can* be aware of. But we are not, or at least do not appear to be, aware of such judgments. Nor does it appear possible for us to be conscious of many of the sorts of activities Descartes attributes to the mind when using the homunculus model—for example, directing our attention out from various points on our retinae.

A final problem is how animals are able to discern the distance, situation, size, and shape of objects. To the extent that any sort of judgment or reasoning is necessarily involved in distance perception, it would follow that animals could not perceive distance. And if the standard interpretation of Descartes' view of animals is correct[30]—namely, that they lack any sort of consciousness at all—then we cannot explain their perceptual abilities by the way God joined the motions in their brains with sensations either.[31] Yet some animals at least are clearly able to tell how far away things are by sight. Since the part of the *Principles* that was to deal with animal perception was never written, we simply do not know how Descartes would have explained this, although there are indications that he saw animal perception operating in much the same way that human perception does, at least for some range of perceptual abilities, since the drawings he uses in the *Dioptrics* were drawn from a sheep's brain. As he explains in a letter to Mersenne in 1637,

> The figure of the brain which I put in the *Dioptrics* is drawn from that of a sheep, of which I know that the ventricles and other interior parts are much larger because of all of the mass of the brain, than in that of a man; but I judged it even more appropriate for this subject to make it possible to see that of which I was speaking, which is common to beasts and men; for I did not suppose anything new or controversial in anatomy.[32]

When Descartes employs the drawing in the *Dioptrics*, he is talking about the physiology of the visual system, and therefore it follows that he believes that the basic physiological mechanisms he describes there are "common to beasts and men." How, then, does a sheep perceive the distance of objects? Even those who contend that Descartes does not deny consciousness to animals,[33] or that Descartes need not have denied consciousness to animals and had no good reason to do so,[34] still do not contend that Descartes believes animals to be capable of making judgments of the sort he ascribes to the human soul in his discussion of spatial perception. So how *do* animals perceive the spatial properties of objects? Or if we suppose that a wholly mechanistic explanation *could* be given for animal perception,[35] then it would be unnecessary to postulate judgment in the human case. The problem of animal perception becomes even more acute in his account of perception in the Sixth Replies, since the homunculus model becomes more prominent there, and I return to it again in the conclusion, since I believe it lies close to one of the main fault lines in Descartes' system and touches on one of the things that is most deeply at issue between Descartes and the Aristotelians.

Replies to Sixth Set of Objections

The objections to the *Meditations* obliged Descartes to confront questions about perception different from those in his earlier writings. Epistemological issues concerning certainty and error come to the fore, as does the broader issue of the role of the senses in knowledge. Indeed, the attempt to wean people away from reliance on their senses as sources of knowledge is one of the central themes of the *Meditations*—and one that elicits opposition particularly from the Aristotelians.

One of the authors of the Sixth Set of Objections, for example, expresses concern about Descartes' mistrust of the senses and his belief that the reliability of the intellect is greater than that of the senses. From the Aristotelian point of view, of course, the certainty of the intellect is built on that of the senses, and to undercut their reliability would be to undermine any knowledge our intellect has constructed on this basis. Our being able to correct for the deceptive appearance of a stick partially submerged in water is, the objector argues, not a function of our intellect; our sense of touch corrects for the error of sight.[36]

Descartes disagrees with this and argues that only the intellect can correct for the misleading appearance of the stick, and in the course of his argument, he draws a very sharp distinction between sensation and judgment—indeed, far sharper than in the *Dioptrics*. And his account here diverges in other important respects from his earlier one.

I begin with a brief summary of Descartes' account of the three levels of sense in the Sixth Replies and then answer several questions about it:

1. How does it differ from his account in the *Dioptrics*?
2. To what extent has it succeeded in resolving problems left unresolved by his earlier account?
3. To what extent has it exacerbated his earlier problems or created new ones?
4. Does it provide a more satisfactory account overall?

Descartes distinguishes three levels or grades of sensory response. The lowest includes only physical motions in the organs, while the second

comprises all the immediate effects produced in the mind as a result of its being united with a bodily organ which is affected in this way. Such effects include the perceptions of pain, pleasure, thirst, hunger, colours, sound, taste, smell, heat, cold and the like, which arise from the union and as it were the intermingling of mind and body.[37]

If taken at face value, this list implies that Descartes intends to limit the second level of sense purely to sensory qualities. The second grade of sensation in the case of vision, then, "extends to the mere perception of the colour and light reflected from the stick,"[38] and nothing more than this should be referred to the sensory faculty. Strictly speaking, no falsity, Descartes says, occurs at this level.

The third level includes all the judgments we have habitually made from our youth and so is not properly a kind of sensation at all; we merely take it to be a form of sensation because the judgments are made so quickly and habitually that we do not notice them. Descartes then goes on to attribute a number of things to this sort of judgment. He says:

> But suppose that, as a result of being affected by this sensation of color, I judge that a stick, located outside of me, is colored; and suppose that on the basis of the extension of the color and its boundaries together with its position [*situation* in French and *situ* in Latin] in relation to the parts of the brain, I make a rational calculation about the size, shape and distance of the stick: although such reasoning is commonly assigned to the senses (which is why I have here referred it to the third grade of sensory response) it is clear that it depends solely on the intellect. I demonstrated in the *Optics* how size, distance and shape can be perceived by reasoning alone, which works out any one feature from the other features.[39]

In spite of his claim that he is only reiterating what he says in the *Dioptrics*, the picture presented here is in some respects very different from the one provided in the *Dioptrics*. For one thing, the role of judgment here is clearly larger than it is in the earlier works. Even perceiving the stick as external ("located outside me") is said to involve judgment. In the *Dioptrics*, Descartes does not take our perception of objects as external to us to require explanation. It is, after all, through the skeptical doubts of the *Meditations* that the externality of the things we perceive is thrown into question. *All* perception of distance, size, and shape is now said to involve "rational calculation," which is not true in the *Dioptrics*, at least for distance perception.

Another difference is that situation perception, central as it is in the *Dioptrics*, is not explained at all. Does it belong to the second level or the third level? It does not fit on the second level (being by no stretch of the imagination a sensory quality), but it is presupposed by the third level. Since situation perception is so fundamental to visual spatial perception, no account that fails to explain it can be a satisfactory one.

Descartes' omission of situation perception is symptomatic of a deeper change—namely, his complete omission of our awareness of the spatiality of our own body as a significant factor in visual spatial perception. With it goes the assimilation of vision to touch that plays such an important role in Descartes' earlier discussion of distance and situation perception. To adapt a theological term, one could say that Descartes' earlier account is more incarnational than his later, in that the close interweaving of body and soul is stressed there more. In line with this downplaying of the role of the body, those means of distance perception that do not involve a clear, rational calculation (e.g., changes in eye shape) drop out, signaling a movement in the direction of involving the homunculus model in all perception.

Given, then, that Descartes makes significant changes from his earlier to his later account, the question arises of the extent to which these changes resolve the problems left outstanding by the *Dioptrics*. One thing Descartes does seem to try to clarify is the nature of the corrective judgments involved in vision. As I have shown, these are problematic both because the special status of the retinal and/ or pineal gland images is not clearly explained and because the nature of these judgments is obscure—are they conscious or not?

The Sixth Replies does not fully clarify the status of the retinal image or its pineal correlate. It is natural to read Descartes as believing that what is given on the second level of sensation is, in the case of vision, a pattern of light and color structurally isomorphic with the retinal image, but he does not explicitly *say* this. It is, however, hard to see what else it could be, since colors are perceived as spread out in space and not as all-pervasive like odors, and on the basis of his physiological theory we would naturally expect them to be arranged as they are in the retinal image. Descartes does, however, do better when it comes to clarifying the problem of whether the corrective judgments are conscious or not.

He notes that "from our earliest years we have made judgments, or even rational inferences about the things which affect our senses." The first time we make such a judgment we attribute it to the intellect, but we learn to "make the calculation and judgment at great speed because of habit, or rather we remember the judgments we have long made about similar objects; and so we do not distinguish these operations from simple sense-perception."[40] Descartes seems, thus, to be moving in the direction of the sort of sensory core theory we find used by Locke where we do initially perceive a kind of mental copy of the retinal image, but the mind makes various corrective judgments so habitually and quickly that we fail even to notice the underlying sensory core and perceive objects in their true situations and distances and with their correct sizes and shapes[41] (although Descartes has a more rationalistic conception of the nature of the corrective judgments—a kind of rational calculation occurs,[42] and not merely an habitual association of ideas).[43] The judgments involved are ones of which we could be aware, but usually are not.

This position is, however, subject to serious objections. It does not seem true that we can, in fact, be aware of such judgments even if we try. And in any case, judgments of which we are not aware simply do not fit with Descartes' equation of the mental with the conscious. The suggestion that we merely "remember the judgments we have long made about similar objects"[44] seems intended to account for the fact that we find ourselves unable to catch ourselves making such judgments, but what does it mean to remember a judgment? More needs to be said.

Stressing the ubiquitousness of judgments in perception does have one advantage for Descartes in that it helps him to reconcile our perceptual errors with God's benevolence, since our errors about distance, size, and shape result from incorrect judgments on our part and thus are our fault and not God's. This has some odd consequences. Curiously enough, in light of Descartes' ambitions in physics and the way in which size and shape are basic elements of that physics, we are necessarily fallible in the judgments we make about these (since they belong to the third level). We are, perhaps, less fallible when we make a judgment for the first time and are, therefore, explicitly conscious of the reasoning involved, but it is only at the second level that no falsity can occur, and this is of no use at all for physics.

The problems raised above in relation to the *Dioptrics* about whether both the mechanical and the homunculus models are operative in all perception and whether the homunculus model is eliminable in principle are not addressed directly, but it does appear that both are involved in virtually all perception, since Descartes takes even our perception of the externality of the stick to involve judgment. The second level must be temporally prior, however, since it is "on the basis of" the extension of the color that I make the judgments about the stick. Descartes, thus, shows no inclination to eliminate the homunculus model in favor of more complex mechanical explanations but, rather, extends the role of judgments and rational calculations by the mind.

This, however, actually exacerbates the problem Descartes already had in his earlier works with explaining animal perception. Given the larger role attributed to reasoning by the mind, explaining how animals can perceive the spatial qualities of objects has become far more difficult. Working out distance, size, and shape reciprocally from each other involves some fairly complex mathematics (a fact that leads Malebranche to suppose that God must make such judgments in and for us). Animals, at least according to the position he takes in the Sixth Replies, have only what Descartes describes as the first level of sensation—namely, the physical motions in the organs. Yet they often discern the spatial location of things as well as and better than we do. And if the ability to discriminate situation, distance, size, and shape can be explained completely mechanistically in animals, the problem arises again of why must we invoke reasoning and judgment in the human case?

Is there any reason to prefer the account of visual perception given in the Sixth

Replies over that given in the *Dioptrics*? Since the Sixth Replies was written later it might seem logical to suppose it is more representative of Descartes' mature thought and therefore supersedes the earlier account. There are several problems with assuming this, however. First Descartes continues to refer his readers to the *Dioptrics* for his account of vision, so he clearly does not regard it as superseded.[45]

The main reason not to rely too heavily on the Sixth Replies, however, is that there are some very serious internal problems with Descartes' account there that make it hard to make sense of it at all, let alone to rest very much weight on it. The actual mechanism he describes is most peculiar. He says that I make a judgment "on the basis of the extension of the color and its boundaries together with its position in relation to the parts of the brain." But which color are we talking about—the experienced color (which is presumably a sensation and not in space) or the color in or on the object? In neither case does it really make sense to talk about its position in relation to the *parts of my brain*. Which parts? How? In his earlier account, Descartes at least provides an explanation involving the mind transferring its attention out from various body parts. The kind of implicit triangulation he postulates in the *Dioptrics* functions because we know how far apart our eyes are and in which direction they are turned. But Descartes cannot rely on this in the Replies to the Sixth Objections, since our awareness of the spatiality of our own bodies has dropped completely out of his account. And no plausible alternative mechanism is presented. To be aware of the spatial position of the parts of our own brain is probably impossible, and it would not help us perceive the distance of objects if we could.

Worse yet, there appears to be a circularity in his explanation. According to Descartes, I already have to know the "position" (*situation, situ*) of the extension of the color "relative to the parts of my brain" in order to calculate its size, shape and distance. But surely it is illegitimate to assume that we already know its position relative to the parts of our brain when we are trying to explain how we visually perceive its spatial location. Descartes assumes what he is trying to explain, or at least one very important component of it. The Sixth Replies, thus, does not stand on its own as an adequate explanation of visual spatial perception.

Conclusion

The problem of visual spatial perception presents serious difficulties for Descartes' project of providing a wholly mechanistic account of vision. The basic core mechanism of vision, as explained in chapter 3, comes very close to providing what he wants—a kind of mechanized Aristotelianism that conveys the figure of the object seen (rather than its "form") to the soul at the pineal gland. But it does not account for how the defects of that image (two-dimensionality, inversion, perspective distortions, etc.) are corrected for, and Descartes does not succeed in providing any mechanistic explanation that he finds completely satisfactory. Although he attempts to do so for situation and distance, shape and especially size perception prove intractable to mechanical explanation within the framework he set out. He thus hypothesizes an increasingly large role for judgments by the mind. This leads to two serious problems. First, if the mind is to correct for defects in the retinal image—for example, to make calculations about the real size of an object based on its size in the retinal image compared with our beliefs about its distance—then it must logically have access of some sort to the retinal image. And there seems to be no way Descartes can account for this without falling into illegitimately thinking of the soul as gazing at the retinal image like the man in the dark room or else by adopting a form of the sensory core theory according to which the sensory core is a mental copy of the retinal image and all other aspects of our visual experience are the result of judgments we make so quickly and habitually as not to notice them. But this fits poorly with Descartes' equation of mind with consciousness, for how can we make judgments of which we have no awareness at all (especially since many of them involve complex mathematics)?

Second, the problem of animals' visual spatial perception is insoluble if judgment or reasoning is necessary to account for the perception of distance, size, and shape by sight. According to the Sixth Replies, all animals possess is the first grade of sensory response, and if their often very acute visual perceptual abilities can be explained with no reference either to conscious sensations (second level) or to judgments (third level), then why not do the same for human visual spatial perception? Insofar as the *Dioptrics* account emphasizes judgment less, animal perception is less of a problem to explain, but even there some element of judgment cannot be eliminated.

Conclusion

DESCARTES' INNOVATIONS IN EXPLAINING VISION INVOLVE BOTH NEW IDEAS about the actual structure and function of the visual system and a shift in the basic metaphysical framework within which vision is to be explained. These changes are related. Descartes differs from the Aristotelians in taking the soul to be a substance distinct from the body (the mind being essentially thinking and the body essentially extension), in believing it to interact with the body only at the pineal gland, and in proposing to treat the body as a machine. If the soul is acted on by the body only at the pineal gland, then information about the visual world must be conveyed to the pineal gland. The mechanism of transmission is, Descartes believes, the projection of a pattern of motions structurally isomorphic with the retinal image into the brain, and so to account for our vision of a unified object, he supposes that the images from the two eyes are merged at the pineal gland.

This general picture of the visual process (minus some of his more quixotic hypotheses about animal spirits) is generally accepted by his successors, and as a result, they, consciously or unconsciously having vision in mind when they discuss perception, face different problems in the philosophy of perception than Descartes' predecessors. Descartes' theory of vision is, thus, one of those places where philosophy turns a corner.

Descartes' work on color led his successors to debate whether colors are to be identified with configurations of particles in motion at the surfaces of objects, with motions of light particles, with sensations in the mind, or perhaps with some sort of powers in the objects to produce sensations in us. But the assumption common to the Aristotelians that objects in the world have the qualities our senses discern in them was gone, and Descartes' successors had to radically rethink the role of the senses in obtaining knowledge about the world in light of the gulf thus created between the world as we experience it by the senses and the world as it really is.[1] Although Descartes' own view of colors is not as idealistic as that of Malebranche or Berkeley, his radical dualism and mechanistic view of nature do pave the way for an idealistic view of colors.

Descartes' successors struggle also with the sort of "veil of perception" skepticism that raises the question of how we can know that there is an external world since we immediately perceive only ideas. Locke and Berkeley talk about how we immediately perceive only ideas because Descartes' theory of vision paves the way for this view. Several features of Descartes' theory fed into it.

First, Descartes' dualism makes the mind, as subject, confront the brain as an object. Hence, there is an inner object of perception in at least one sense. Second, his understanding of the role of the retinal image in vision involves an inner object (the pattern of motions traced at the surface of the pineal gland) that actually even resembles the external object (although imperfectly) by being structurally isomorphic with it. In addition, his explanation of visual spatial perception is based on the presupposition that the soul has some sort of access to the retinal image or its pineal correlate. And finally, the retinal image serves as a kind of imaginative model of an idea. The notion that we immediately or directly perceive some sort of inner object is intuitively plausible only for vision; we think of vision as analogous to perception by means of pictures or images. But it is very difficult even to imagine what it could be for the other senses to give us indirect access to their objects in this sort of way.

The Aristotelian framework does not tend to generate this particular form of skepticism.[2] Not knowing about the existence of the retinal image, of course, prevented the Aristotelians from making some of the mistakes about its role in vision that Descartes makes. But there are also reasons inherent in their metaphysical framework. Aristotelians think in terms of a hierarchy of powers possessed by living things rather than the mind confronting or interacting with the body. And understanding visual perception as involving the reception of "forms" or "species" has several advantages over Descartes' corresponding term *figure*. First, the pattern of figures and motions that Descartes believes is transmitted from the retina to the pineal gland is material and so cannot exist in the mind and establish a unity of knower and known as did the forms or intentional species of the tradition. And, second, since the Aristotelian explanation in terms of the reception of forms remains at a highly abstract level of analysis, it could, I think, be argued that this makes it easier to escape from the necessity of postulating resembling images. To say that the sense faculty is taking on the form of the sense object is not yet to say anything about exactly what physical processes are occurring, and thus, forms allow for more flexibility than Descartes' notion of figure.

A third problem that engages the attention of Descartes' immediate successors is distinguishing what is properly "given" to the sense of sight from those aspects of our visual experience added by the mind through judgment, association of ideas, etc. In drawing this distinction between seeing and judging (which they do more sharply than Descartes himself), they rely on his theory of vision, concluding that the sensory given for vision is a two-dimensional mosaic of light and colors structurally isomorphic with the retinal image.[3] They do not rely merely on introspection, since size, shape, and distance appear to be just as much given to sight as colors, and they could not rely on the visual experience of infants, since we cannot communicate with infants.[4] The Aristotelians draw the distinction between seeing and judging along very different lines and assign to the common sense many of the functions that Descartes' theory assigns to judgments by the mind.

Descartes makes genuine advances in explaining vision, and his theory is historically of great importance for the demise of Aristotelianism and to the genesis of early modern theories of perception. But he can be criticized from two directions. First, Descartes' theory suffers from some serious unclarities and inner tensions; and second, modern scientific discoveries about vision do not bear out some of his central ideas.

The retinal image and its pineal correlate clearly have a privileged status in vision for Descartes, but he never adequately clarifies this status. Explaining visual spatial perception puts a strain on his theory, which he tries to handle either by utilizing a kind of inner object of vision that threatens to entangle him in an infinite regress or by retreating in various ways from his official dualism or from the belief that the mind interacts with the body only at the pineal gland. In the *Dioptrics* especially, he sometimes lapses into seeing the mind as somehow spread throughout (or informing) the body, thus enabling the mind to be present in the eyes or hands to know (*connaître*—be acquainted with) the places where they are and to direct its attention out from them. In the *Dioptrics* and even more clearly in the Sixth Replies, Descartes supposes the mind to be performing calculations and making judgments of which we are not aware. But this is impossible within the Cartesian dualistic framework that equates mind with consciousness.

Finally, the problem of how animals perceive distance, size, and shape by sight appears insoluble in light of the fact that such perception requires judgment, according to Descartes. Since animals manifest the ability to make many of the same perceptual discriminations we do, and since Descartes supposes that the basic anatomy of the visual system does not differ radically between, say, a person and a sheep,[5] why should we treat the two cases in a radically different way? If we can explain these sorts of perception mechanistically in sheep, why invoke judgment in the human case? Or if we need judgment in the human case, why not concede that sheep also make judgments?

Explaining the area of overlap between human perceptual abilities and those of animals is not a problem in the same way for the Aristotelians because of their belief in the sensitive soul and its persistence in human beings as a faculty of the rational soul. An Aristotelian would not be troubled by the suggestion that animals possess awareness and even a kind of rudimentary sort of knowledge[6] because they believe that the common sense performs many of the functions in both animals and humans that Descartes ascribes to judgments by the mind. Spatial perception would doubtless be one such function.[7]

Descartes, however, rejects the sensitive soul altogether, regarding animal souls as in the same general category as "other forms and qualities."[8] An animal's soul would be, of course, the substantial form of the animal, but Descartes does not believe that they have substantial souls. Their souls are not distinct from blood, heat, and spirits.[9] And according to Descartes, the sensitive power in man is nothing but a certain arrangement of the parts of the body.[10]

Descartes' rejection of the notion of the sensitive soul would seem to imply that any sort of consciousness for animals is impossible, but oddly enough, I believe it would be easier for him to admit that animals have consciousness or thought than to allow them sensitive souls, and in several passages, he appears either to ascribe consciousness to animals or at least to leave open the possibility.[11] His considered view, however, is quite clearly that that they do not possess thought (*cogitationem*,[12] *pensée* or *entendment*[13]). And even if they did, they certainly do not possess the powers of reason and judgment Descartes employs in his account of visual spatial perception. Animal perception, therefore, resists explanation in a way consistent with the rest of Descartes' system.

There are a number of moves Descartes could make in order to attempt to resolve the problem.[14] But these would involve changes elsewhere in his system, which Descartes might well resist making,[15] and to provide a rational reconstruction of Descartes' views about animals goes beyond the scope of the present work. Work would need to be done on the actual perceptual abilities of animals as well as on the conceptual resources Descartes has to account for them. For our purposes, it is sufficient to note that Descartes' theory of vision, as articulated in the texts considered here, cannot account for the fact that some animals at least are able to make the same sorts of perceptual discriminations we are.

Descartes' theory of vision is open not only to internal critique but also to critique in terms of the outcome of the scientific revolution he helped to foster. One important point on which modern science has not supported Descartes' theory of vision is his understanding of the role of the retinal image in vision. Although the retinal images are projected into the brain, they are never actually merged. They are projected to several different areas of the brain and are subject to topological distortion. The eyes are in constant rapid motion so that the image projected on the retina changes constantly while our visual field remains stable.[16] Thus, although the retinal image still retains a central role in vision, that role must be quite unlike the one envisioned by Descartes.

Certainly Descartes should not be faulted for being ignorant of modern neurophysiology. He had to think about vision in terms of familiar things, such as simple machines or the camera obscura. But at the same time, it would seem that if Descartes' hypotheses about vision had such an important influence on the directions taken by early modern perceptual theory, then modifying or replacing them will have implications for issues in the philosophy of perception, such as whether and how it is possible to get back to some sort of sensory "given," what is the ontological status of colors, and whether or not "veil of perception" skepticism is a serious threat to our claims to knowledge about the world.

It is, of course, too early to know what sort of consensus, if any, will emerge among researchers on visual perception. But certainly one of the possibilities is the reappearance of theories of a broadly Aristotelian sort. The work of the late psychologist J. J. Gibson is a particularly interesting case in point.

Gibson is critical of psychologists who, in the grip of Descartes' mechanistic conception of the body, regard the senses as merely passive channels of sensation. Their focus, like that of Descartes, is on examining the sensory receptors and on tracing how the patterns of excited receptors are projected to the brain, resulting in a stream of sensations out of which the mind (or brain) must somehow construct a stable world. Gibson argues that while these processes do occur, they are not relevant to understanding our perceptual abilities under normal (nonlaboratory) conditions.

Instead of talking about receptors, Gibson prefers to talk about the senses as perceptual systems that actively explore and search out information about the environment present in the patterns of energy in our environment that we detect by the use of our several senses. These patterns do not take the form of "snapshots." They vary over time and change as a result of exploratory movements of our own organism (such as moving, turning the head, etc.), and the regular patterns of change themselves provide important information. What the perceptual systems seek out, he says, are "invarients" (higher order variables of stimulus energy like ratios or proportions, for example), which provide clues to the layout of the surrounding environment.

Although more philosophical work doubtless needs to be done to clarify some of Gibson's terminology (such as "invarients" or "affordances"), his thought is clearly more akin to that of Aristotle than to that of Descartes. For one thing, the senses are no longer regarded as passive or as yielding simply snapshots or unconnected atoms of sensation, but rather as active and possessing a kind of built-in purposiveness. Also, his emphasis, like that of Aristotle, is on structural features of our world to which we try to attune ourselves.

In the end, Descartes' two theories of vision—the mechanical and the homuncular—succeed neither singly nor in combination. For all that, Descartes' work on vision is an important and influential chapter in the history of modern philosophy and science.

NOTES

BIBLIOGRAPHY

INDEX

NOTES

The following abbreviations will appear in the notes to indicate the editions of Descartes' works:

A   *Oeuvres philosophiques*. Ed. with annotations by Ferdinand Alquié. 3 vols. Paris: Classiques Garnier, Editions Garnier Frères, 1967.

AT   *Oeuvres de Descartes*. Ed. by Charles Adam and Paul Tannery. Rev. ed. 12 vols. Paris: Librairie Philosophique, J. Vrin/C.N.R.S., 1964–76.

CSM   *Philosophical Writings of Descartes*. Trans. by John Cottingham, Robert Stroothoff, and Dugald Murdoch. 2 vols. Cambridge: Cambridge Univ. Press, 1985.

HR   *Philosophical Works of Descartes*. Trans. by Elizabeth Haldane and G. R. T. Ross. 2 vols. Cambridge: Cambridge Univ. Press, 1973.

K   *Descartes' Philosophical Letters*. Trans. by Anthony Kenny. Oxford: Clarendon, 1970.

O   *Discourse on Method, Optics, Geometry and Meteorology*. Trans. by Paul Olscamp. New York: Bobbs-Merrill, 1965.

Introduction

1. For an interesting discussion of this, see Larmore.
2. See Maull.
3. Arbini, 317–18.
4. Wilson, "Descartes on the Perception of Primary Qualities," 18.
5. This sort of view is usually called the "sensory core" theory. See, e.g., Hatfield and Epstein.
6. On the issue of representationalism, see, e.g., Arbini; Cook; Lennon; MacKenzie, "Descartes on Sensory Representation"; and Yolton, *Perceptual Aquaintance*.
7. Cook, 179, 182.
8. One could, of course, escape this regress by providing a clear account of "immediate perception" that does not employ terms such as *see, sense,* or *perceive*. But Descartes does not do this.
9. One could, perhaps, arrive at such a view by means of the argument from illusion, but this can be handled without generating a regress by falling back on an adverbial theory of perceiving.
10. This point has often been made, most recently in Rorty's book, *Philosophy and the Mirror of Nature*. He believes that this visual metaphor has generated all sorts of deep errors and must be discarded. Some feminists of late have also decried the pervasiveness of visual metaphors in epistemology on the grounds that vision is a peculiarly masculine sense. See, e.g., Grontkowski and Keller.
11. *Principles*, Part IV, 188; AT, IX2:310; CSM, I:279. Quotations from works of Descartes will be cited by title.
12. Sixth Replies, AT, VII:435; CSM, II:293.
13. See Ronchi, 119.
14. A mechanistic account of light would be, of course, even more unacceptable to those within the Neoplatonic tradition. For an interesting discussion of the metaphysical and epistemological significance of light metaphors in ancient and medieval thought, see Lindberg's introduction to his translation of Bacon's *On the Multiplication of Species*, xxxv–liii. In attempting to mechanize light, Descartes is going against what seems to be a perennial tendency of the human mind to think of light as somehow immaterial or spiritual. This is especially true within the Platonic and Christian traditions but by no means limited to them.
15. *Dioptrics*, AT, VI:85; O, 68. It should be noted that Descartes did not take the theory that these species "fly through the air" to be the view of Aristotle, or even of all scholastic philosophers, for he attributes belief in "intentional forms" to "many philosophers" immediately after he has been

referring to Aristotle's views in the Fourth Replies (AT, VII:249; CSM, II:174). Had he taken the view to be that of Aristotle, he would have had no reason not to say so.

16. See, e.g., Sixth Replies, AT, VII:435; CSM, II:293; *Meteorology*, AT, VI:331; O, 336; *Passions of the Soul* I, 12, and I, 13, AT, XI:337–38; *Treatise on Man*, AT, XI:153, 156; *Principles*, Part IV, 189, AT, IX2:310; author's letters to translator of *Principles*, AT, IX2:15; HR, I:212; *Comments on a Certain Broadsheet*, AT, VIIIB:359; CSM, I:304).

17. *Discourse*, AT, VI:75–77; HR, I:127–29.

18. Fortunately, this seems to be the case less now than it was. See, e.g., the works of Carriero, Hatfield, and Garber.

19. AT, III:185.

20. See, e.g., Wells' arguments to the effect that Francisco Suarez was particularly influential on Descartes' thought in "Objective Reality of Ideas" and "Material Falsity."

21. See, e.g., Ariew's articles, "Descartes and Scholasticism" and "Early Seventeenth-Century Philosophy"; de Rochemonteix; and Sirven. For further information on the textbook tradition in particular, see Reif; Schmitt, "The Rise of the Philosophical Textbook"; and Wallace, "Traditional Natural Philosophy."

22. Wallace, "Traditional Natural Philosophy," 204.

23. A point he makes much of in the *Discourse*. See, e.g., AT, VI:8–9; CSM, I:114–15.

24. AT, III:231–32.

25. An interesting discussion of the diversity of late scholasticism is found in Mercer's essay "The Vitality and Importance of Early Modern Aristotelianism."

26. Cited by Ariew in "Descartes and Scholasticism," 9–11.

27. For example, a group of scholars who put forward anti-Aristotelian theses in 1624 were officially condemned and exiled. Cited by Garber in "Descartes, the Aristotelians and the Revolution," 477.

28. Descartes himself cites Aristotle's works and tries where possible to downplay his differences from him. See, e.g., his letter to Fr. Charlet, an influential Jesuit, where he speaks of how "passionately" he desires the friendship of the Jesuits, since they have the power to impede his philosophy from even getting a hearing or to bring about its success by supporting it, and he goes on to claim that his new philosophy (or parts of it at least) can be taught in the schools "without contradicting the text of Aristotle" (AT, IV:157).

29. This is not to say, however, that he regretted having been educated in scholastic philosophy at La Flèche. Indeed, he believed he had received an excellent philosophical education there and recommended it to a friend as the best place to send his son. See AT, II:378.

30. AT, III:297–98; K, 94.

31. AT, III:470.

32. He is able to make such a distinction, however. See, e.g., his remark in the introduction to the French edition of the *Principles* about the philosophers who corrupted the sense of Aristotle's writings and "attributed to him various opinions which he would not recognize to be his, were he now to return to this world" (AT, IX:7; CSM, I:182). While this does not prove he always distinguished accurately between Aristotle and the later scholastics, it does prove that he sometimes did.

33. I do not mean to suggest that nobody held such a view. The Renaissance had seen a revival of Democritean-Epicurean theories of sense perception (Popkin, 677), and certainly some of Descartes' contemporaries had a tendency to reify species (on this see Reif and Miles). But species were standardly held to be accidents and not substances, so it is not correct to interpret the scholastics in general as holding the view that species fly off objects and travel through the air in such a way that actual matter passes from the object to us.

1. Descartes' Thought about Perception in Rule XII

1. Marion, *Sur l'ontologie grise de Descartes*, 186.

2. *Rules*, AT, X:369; CSM, I:14.

3. There are "more historical filiations, all things considered, between Descartes and Aristotle than between Descartes and the neoscholastics (the *Rules* take scarcely any notice of those opinions held specifically by recent thinkers, and go so far as to explicitly repudiate the authors of later years)" ([translation mine] Marion, *Sur l'ontologie grise de Descartes*, 23).

4. Aristotle, *De Anima*, 412a27–30. This citation and subsequent citations in text of the *De Anima* are to the translation by J. A. Smith, *The Works of Aristotle*, vol. 3, and are designated *DA* when necessary.

5. There is some discrepancy between the *De Anima* and his more physiological texts on this point. This point is discussed further in chapter 3 of this book.

6. Eustace of St. Paul, who I take to be generally representative of the textbook tradition, says, "Soul is the act of a natural organic body having life in potency" and is "that whereby primarily we live, feel and know" (248–49). And even the more ecclectic textbooks, such as that of Dupleix, repeat Aristotle's definition (see 359 and 361).

7. In the sixteenth century many philosophers moved in the direction of identifying the soul and its faculties, although many still clung to Thomistic faculty psychology—particularly in Jesuit circles, for example, the Coimbra *De Anima* author. On this point, see Park, 477–81. Dupleix, in his summary of scholastic philosophy, treats the issue of how the faculties relate to the soul as controversial but favors the Thomistic understanding of the nutritive and sensitive souls as "faculties" of the intellectual soul and argues against speaking of the lower souls as contained "eminently" in the higher (363–72).

8. Eustace takes up this question and argues that they are not in the soul but in the body but then notes that the subject of faculties is "not merely the body but the animated body," which means, of course, the body informed by the soul (262).

9. Many writers adopted a theory of successive ensoulment, for example, Dupleix, 363–72.

10. This complex interplay of activity and passivity is preserved in the accounts of standard textbooks of Descartes' time. See, e.g., Eustace, 290.

11. See Garber, "Descartes, the Aristotelians, and the Revolution," for a discussion of the way in which many of Descartes' contemporaries regarded him as simply reviving the doctrines of the ancient atomists rather than perceiving his originality.

12. See, e.g., Eustace, 290–93 and 318. But the more ecclectic textbook of Dupleix employs the term *image* (in French) instead of *species*, although he does use the term *species* occasionally (e.g., 438). Interestingly, the term *species* was used in explaining vision, even when it had been dropped for the other senses (Park, 481).

13. For an interesting discussion of this, see O'Neil's "Direct Realism and Sensory Abstraction."

14. Aquinas, Quodlibetum V q.5 a2, ad2, trans. by Peifer, 99.

15. Aquinas, *Summa Theologica*, Ia, Q78, a3.

16. Park notes this for the Renaissance in general (470), and certainly the fourteenth century was a time of great interest in the epistemological issues involved in perception. (See also Tachau for a valuable discussion of these.)

17. Thomists, elaborating on the texts of St. Thomas, developed a complex theory of intentional causality, in which the medium, due to the intentional presence within it of the celestial bodies and the separated substances, was able somehow to spiritualize the species passing through it, so that it could act upon the soul of the perceiver. For a good discussion of the doctrine of intentionality in St. Thomas and some of his followers, see Hayen's book. On the problem of intentionality in the external senses, see esp. 127–39.

18. Thomas had said that "the sense, itself, does not produce any sensible form," and John of St. Thomas (trying to prevent the emergence of any sort of representative entity in sense perception) argued that: "The external senses do not form an image, but are immediately terminated at the object as it is itself" (*Cursus Philosophicus*, III:172, cited in Peifer, 99). Other philosophers, especially those who emphasized the corporeal nature of the species in the medium, e.g., Ruvio, held that the external senses do produce an expressed species.

19. Park, 480.

20. Ross, *Aristotle*, 140.

21. For an interesting discussion of Aristotle's theory of imagination, see Bundy, chap. 3.

22. I discuss this issue in more detail in chapter 3.

23. Aristotle, *De Memoria*, 450a 26-b 13, trans. by J. I. Beare, *The Works of Aristotle*, vol. 3.

24. For a valuable discussion of the historical evolution of theories about the internal senses, see Wolfson.

25. Aquinas discusses the interior senses at *Summa Theologica*, Ia, Q.78, a4. The discursive power has been of interest to subsequent Thomists, who in the wake of Cartesianism have been trying to examine the point at which the sense powers interface with the intellect. Some hold that it occurs at the common sense, and some hold that it is the cogitative or discursive power. For the latter position, see Klubertanz.

26. Park, 480–81. Thus Eustace, for example, after citing various conflicting opinions, adopts the view that all the internal senses are properly forms of phantasia (316), while Dupleix opts for only the three mentioned by Aristotle (439–43).

27. The reason why Aristotle needs to postulate an active intellect and Plato does not, he says, is because Plato believed the essences of sensible things existed apart from matter in a state of actual intelligibility, whereas Aristotle denied this. And the essences of sensible things so long as they exist in matter are only potentially intelligible. It is the active intellect, then, that abstracts such intelligible forms or species from the phantasms so that they can be received by the passive intellect, which then generates a universal concept, sometimes called the expressed intelligible species or the word.

28. The Thomist position here was that they were. Toletus and de Goes held back from firmly asserting this, and Toletus even went so far as to concede probability to the position that there is only one intellectual potency in the soul, which is both active and passive, but nonetheless took the agent intellect to be necessary in explaining cognition (Kessler, 511–13).

29. Thomists answered this in the negative, but the Scotists said yes, and commentators Descartes read, such as Toletus and de Goes, either inclined toward the Scotists or accepted both positions as defensible (Kessler, 512–23).

30. See Kessler's article "The Intellective Soul" for a good summary of the positions taken on all these issues by the major philosophical schools in the sixteenth and early seventeenth centuries.

31. The active intellect and passive intellect appear, for example, in such textbooks of the time as Eustace, 336–41, and Dupleix, 447–48.

32. Rule XII, AT, X:412–13; CSM, I:40.

33. Rule XII, AT, X:412; CSM, I:40.

34. Rule XII, AT, X:412; CSM, I:40.

35. Rule XII, AT, X:412–13; CSM, I:40.

36. Rule XII, AT, X:413; CSM, I:41.

37. *Descartes' Rules for Direction of the Mind*, trans. by La Fleur, 46.

38. Rule XII, AT, X:414; CSM, I:41.

39. Interestingly, this parallels the Thomistic account where the imagination uses the same species as the common sense. See Peifer, 105.

40. Rule XII, AT, X:414; CSM, I:41–42.

41. Rule XII, HR, I:38.

42. Roy, for example, argues that Descartes is trying to elevate figure to be something quasi-spiritual in these passages (16–25).

43. *Treatise on Man*, AT, XI:176–77.

44. O'Neil calls the result "a physicalistic version of the Aristotelian/scholastic theory" (*Epistemological Direct Realism*, 3) and believes that Descartes was at the time he wrote the *Rules* "still working within an essentially traditional or scholastic framework" (54). As I argue in this chapter, however, I believe his departures from the traditional theory are already too great to regard him as working within that framework.

45. Rule XII, AT, X:415; CSM, I:42.

46. This point is also made by Beck, *The Method of Descartes*, 29; and by O'Neil, *Epistemological Direct Realism*, 74.

47. Rule XII, AT, X:415; CSM, I:42.

48. *Dioptrics*, AT, VI:130; O, 101.

49. For an interesting contrast between Descartes' view of the understanding in Rule XII and Aristotle's view of *nous*, see Marion, *Sur l'ontologie grise de Descartes*, 126–31.

50. Quotations in this paragraph are from Rule XII, AT, X:415–16; CSM, I:42–43.
51. Rule XII, AT, X:416–17; CSM, I:43.
52. Rule XII, AT, X:423; CSM, I:47.

2. Descartes' Theory of Light and Color

1. Descartes, however, is not entirely consistent on this point. See *Dioptrics*, AT, VI:86; O, 68.

2. In this he differs radically from Newton, who sees that white light is, itself, a heterogeneous mixture of rays that differ in refrangibility, reflexibility, and in the color they exhibit. For a valuable discussion of the way in which Descartes' understanding of color remains within the Aristotelian tradition by contrast with that of Newton, see Westfall.

3. This citation and subsequent citations in text are to J. I. Beare's translation of *De Sensu et Sensibili*, *The Works of Aristotle*, vol. 3, and are designated *DS* when necessary.

4. Lindberg's works are particularly helpful for understanding the history of optics during the Middle Ages and the Renaissance, and Ronchi's history of light is also a classic. Tachau's book is a very valuable source for discussion of the epistemological issues in fourteenth-century optics.

5. AT, II:86.

6. Whether Kepler's work should be viewed as a culmination of that tradition or whether he was a revolutionary figure who transformed the tradition by mechanizing it is a question disputed by experts in the history of optics. Lindberg, in particular, argues for the view that Kepler was the culminating figure in the perspectivist tradition in his book *Theories of Vision From Al-Kindi to Kepler*, while Crombie, in "The Mechanistic Hypothesis," emphasizes the mechanistic elements in Kepler. In any case, Kepler certainly drew heavily on perspectivist theories in his own work on the retinal image.

7. I rely largely on A. Mark Smith's research for this list of what Descartes would have read (in *Descartes' Theory of Light and Refraction*, 11–12).

8. This distinction is found, for example, in such textbooks as those of Eustace, 298–99, and Dupleix, 395.

9. The term *species* is not new to him. See Lindberg's introduction to his translation of Bacon's *Multiplication of Species* for a valuable history of the term.

10. See Aquinas, *Commentary on Aristotle's De Sensu* in *In Aristotelis libros De Sens et Sensato*, Lesson V, n. 62.

11. Ockham believed sensible species to be unnecessary and believed he saw serious epistemological dangers in the use of the term. See Tachau, 130–35, for a discussion of Ockham's reasons for rejecting them.

12. Cited in Lindberg, "The Science of Optics," 358.

13. See Hayen, 106–26, for a discussion of the intentionality of light in Thomas and his followers.

14. Cited in Regis, 213.

15. See Hayen, 114.

16. Descartes mentions Ruvio (Rubius) as a scholastic whom he remembers having read at La Flèche (AT, III:185). Ruvio was quite well regarded generally, and his textbook on the *De Anima*, first printed in 1611, would have been the most up-to-date textbook at the time Descartes was a student at La Flèche.

17. Ruvio, *Commentaria in Libros Aristoteles De Anima*, 326.

18. In the *Dioptrics* (AT, VI:85; O, 68), he describes them as "little images flying through the air," and he claims to have delivered us from them immediately after pointing out in his analogy between light and the blind man's stick that nothing material need pass from the object to the eye. He, thus, thinks of intentional species as something material passing from the object to the eye.

19. Aquinas is quite clear that "such things as come to the senses of each individual are not particles flowing out and away from a sensible object," for if perception occurred in this way, it would be impossible for different people to perceive the same object (*Commentary on Aristotle's De Sensu*, Lecture XVI, n. 239).

20. Gilson, *Études*, 25.

21. Eustace defines intentional species as "a formal sign of an object of the senses, of a certain quality, which, once sent by the object and received in the sense has the power to represent this object, though it may be barely perceptible to the sense" (291). But he also speaks of them as "emitted" (302) by objects and of color "sending its species through a medium," and he says that "it cannot be explained how sensation can occur concerning an object which sometimes is very remote unless something is sent by the object to the potency, and unless the faculty itself receives something from the object" (289). While he denies that the species is transmitted "in the manner whereby a lance is sent to a target by a hurler" (291–92), he does seem to accord species a rather odd sort of ghostly being. He says, for example, "It is not sufficient that some light be received in the eye, but it is also required that the species of light be received in the same eye" (240).

22. Reif, 29.

23. Miles, in "Descartes' Mechanism," also notes a tendency in late scholasticism to reify substantial forms and make of them "internal, active causes of motion" (115), like the "little souls" caricatured by Descartes (AT, III:648). Drawing on the work of Anneliese Maier, however, he defends medieval science against many of the accusations commonly made against it by the early moderns.

24. See A. Mark Smith's monograph *Descartes' Theory of Light and Refraction* for an interesting defense of this claim in relation to Descartes' proof of the sine-law.

25. For a valuable discussion of what is in common between Descartes' view of light and that of the perspectivists, see A. Mark Smith's monograph, esp. 45–46. Smith basically tries to do for Descartes what Lindberg does for Kepler—namely, to show how his views grew out of the perspectivist tradition.

26. On this point, see Goddu's review of Smith's monograph.

27. See Park, 480.

28. Dijksterhuis, 414. Other valuable discussions of the nature of Cartesian mechanism (which differ slightly from Dijksterhuis) are in Duhem's *The Evolution of Mechanics* and Mouy's *Le Development de la Physique Cartésienne*.

29. Dijksterhuis, 414. See also Gilson, *Discours de la méthode: texte et commentaire*, 272–73, for a list of the concepts of Aristotelian physics already rejected by Descartes in *The World*.

30. See, e.g., his letter to Mersenne of 1630 in which Descartes already speaks of his physics in terms of a "fable" (AT, I:179).

31. AT, II:368.

32. *Discourse*, AT, VI:18; CSM, I:120.

33. Although as Eastwood argues in "Descartes on Refraction," their pedagogical value is one important reason for their use. Issues about pedagogy were important to Descartes, and he intended in the *Dioptrics* to bypass all the sorts of preliminary studies that would have been required at La Flèche and to address the educated layman with an interest in lens grinding. Imaginative models and diagrams are thus used to substitute for a full discussion of mechanical principles.

34. Clarke (122) seems inclined to attribute this sort of motivation to him.

35. *Rules*, AT, X:416; CSM, I:42.

36. *Rules*, AT, X:417; CSM, I:43.

37. *Rules*, AT, X:416; CSM, I:42.

38. I am indebted for this line of argument to Gaukroger's excellent article "Descartes' Project for a Mathematical Physics," although he does not address the issue of Descartes' use of models.

39. Galison, in "Descartes' Comparisons," correctly rejects attempts to make Descartes' models fit a hypothetical deductive schema and emphasizes (as I do here) the link between Descartes' use of models and the role of the imagination in knowledge, particularly in the epistemology of the *Rules*.

40. *Principles*, AT, IX:321.

41. This is the case even though he described the *Dioptrics* in a letter to Mersenne in 1630 as providing a sort of abridgement of his *World* (AT, I:179).

42. *The World*, AT, XI:24. This and all other quotes from *The World* are my own translations.

43. *The World*, AT, XI:30.

44. *The World*, AT, XI:84.

45. *The World*, AT, XI:84. The next two paragraphs are also based on this section of *The World*, 84–97.

46. *Dioptrics*, AT, VI:83–84; O, 67.

47. *The World*, AT, XI:99.

48. *Dioptrics*, AT, VI:84; O, 67.

49. *Dioptrics*, AT, VI:85; O, 67.

50. *Dioptrics*, AT, VI:85; O, 67.

51. *Dioptrics*, AT, VI:86; O, 68.

52. *Dioptrics*, AT, VI:86; O, 68.

53. Table of the Principal Difficulties, which are explained in the *Dioptrics*, AT, VI:487.

54. *Dioptrics*, AT, VI:87; O, 69.

55. *Treatise on Man*, AT, XI:151.

56. *Meteorology*, AT, VI:331.

57. *Meteorology*, AT, VI:334.

58. Scott, 33.

59. Ronchi, 116.

60. A, I:659.

61. See letter to Mersenne, 5 October 1637, AT, I:450–51; A, I:815–16. See also Wallace, *The Scientific Method of Theodoric*, 262, and Scott, 63, for a discussion of how Descartes responded to Fermat's criticisms of his account of the *matière subtile* involved in the transmission of light.

62. On this point, see Prendergast, 459.

63. As Morin pointed out in his letter of August 1638 (AT, II:291).

64. An assumption Descartes makes explicitly in a letter to Morin (AT, II:367–68), where he says that things too small to be perceived and those that we perceive through our senses do not differ any more from each other than a small circle from a large circle.

65. Consider, for example, the way in which different explanatory principles are employed in quantum mechanics from those used on the level of ordinary perceptible objects.

66. Wallace, *Scientific Methodolgy of Theodoric*, 261.

67. Scott, 23.

68. Gaukroger, "Descartes' Project," 133.

69. Clarke, 122–30 and 197–205.

70. On this topic, see further, Marion's *Sur la théologie blanche de Descartes* and Grene's *Descartes*, chap. 3. And for an interesting discussion of the more general problem of the role of hypotheses in Descartes' physics, see Garber's "Science and Certainty in Descartes" and Larmore.

71. *Dioptrics*, AT, VI:85; O, 66–67.

72. This strategy might well serve Descartes' purposes by encouraging people to look for mechanical explanations instead of the sorts of explanations offered by the Aristotelians, although it might not even achieve this goal if the models are inconsistent with each other in obvious ways. But if Descartes' theory of light is to be the cornerstone of his physics, he surely owes his readers something more than a hodgepodge of mechanistic *virtus dormitiva* explanations.

73. See, e.g., *Discourse*, AT, VI:76; O, 60–61, and his letter to Vatier, AT, I:563.

74. Descartes was aware of and struggling with these sorts of problems. See, for example, his 17 May 1638 letter to Mersenne (AT, II:134; K, 55–56), where he said that he regards his account of refraction in the *Dioptrics* as a demonstration (in some sense) and reiterates his hope of demonstrating the principles of physics by metaphysics. But he also said that we cannot strictly demonstrate the solution to any problem in physics; such proofs are available only in arithmetic and geometry. Exactly how we are to understand what he means by demonstration remains somewhat obscure, especially since he expresses willingness to accept demonstrations based on hypotheses that are uncertain or perhaps even false.

75. See Kemp Smith, *New Studies in the Philosophy*, 24. Crombie also believes that Descartes' work in vision was especially important to the genesis of his mechanism (67).

76. See *De Anima*, 418a10–15, for the claim that color is the special object of vision; *De Sensu*, 439b, for the view that objects partake of color; and for non-reducibility of proper sensibles to common sensibles, see *De Sensu*, 442b.

77. *Dioptrics*, AT, VI:142; CSM, I:173.
78. *Dioptrics*, AT, VI:118; O, 94.
79. AT, III:372–73; K, 103.
80. *Dioptrics*, AT, VI:132; O, 102.
81. *Meteorology*, AT, VI:333–34; O, 337.
82. *Meteorology*, AT, VI:333; O, 337.
83. *Meteorology*, AT, VI:335; O, 338–39.
84. Locke, *Essay*, Book II, II. viii. 23.
85. *The World*, AT, XI:84. Although he insists that no thought or will is involved in this inclination to move, it must be admitted that this sort of tendency appears out of place in his otherwise wholly mechanistic framework.
86. Cottingham's somewhat Lockean reading of Descartes as holding that colors are to be construed as dispositions to set up certain types of motions—in the medium presumably—(Locke would call these tertiary qualities) encounters the same problem as Locke's understanding of them as powers or dispositions to cause sensations in perceivers. If Descartes is to remain a consistent mechanist, dispositions cannot be admitted into his ontology, unless they are identical with the shapes, sizes, motions, and spatial arrangements of the minute parts of matter. And if they are identical with these, then the term *disposition* adds nothing and should be eliminated.
87. Of course, our perceptions of the size or shape of objects are also mental in nature, being modes of our minds.
88. Fourth Replies, AT, VII:254; CSM, II:177.
89. *Description*, AT, XI:256; CSM, I:323. Interestingly, he says that blood *is* red but that hot iron *appears* red. Perhaps red objects are those that impart the requisite motion to light under normal conditions.
90. Sixth Replies, AT, VII:437; CSM, II:294.
91. I use the term *suggests* because it is not *entirely* clear whether "depending on the intellect" is meant to refer only to the latter part of the sentence after the semicolon or to the judgment that the color of the stick is external to me also (although that seems the natural reading).
92. Sixth Replies, AT, VII:437–38; CSM, II:295.
93. *Passions*, AT, XI:338; CSM, I:333.
94. *Passions*, AT, XI:346; CSM, I:337.
95. While he says that ideas of figures and motions are innate, he says that our ideas of "pain, colors, sounds and the like" must be "all the more innate" since they have no resemblance to the motions that cause them (*Comments*, AT, VIIIB:359; CSM, I:304).
96. Berkeley, *Essay*, sec. 79, 203. Our mind reaches only as far as our own ideas and then stops because there is no natural connection between the qualities we experience and anything outside us.

3. The Mechanics of Vision and Our Perception of Light and Color

1. *Dioptrics*, AT, VI:113.
2. Aquinas, *Commentary on Aristotle's De Sensu*, Lesson V, n. 64.
3. Georges-Berthier, 68.
4. Descartes was the first to localize the common sense in a particular part of the brain, and his theory promotes the pineal gland to a new position of primacy—it had previously not been thought to have any particularly important function at all. See Mesnard, 208, for a useful discussion of previous theories about the function of the pineal gland.
5. See Lindberg, *Theories of Vision*, 193–202; and Polyak, 35–36.
6. Rule XII, AT, X:412; CSM, I:40.
7. The following summary is based on *Dioptrics*, AT, VI:114–130; O, 91–100, translations mine.
8. *Dioptrics*, AT, VI:123–24; O, 96–97.
9. For example, at the start of the Sixth Discourse of the *Dioptrics*, he says that "while this picture [*peinture*], in passing thus into the inside of our head, always retains some resemblance to

the objects from which it proceeds, we must nonetheless not be persuaded that it is by means of this that it enables us to sense them, as if there were yet other eyes within our brain with which we could perceive it" (AT, VI:130). The referent of "this" in the phrase "by means of this" is ambiguous. It could refer to either the picture or the resemblance

10. *Dioptrics*, AT, VI:114; O, 91.

11. See, e.g., *Dioptrics,* AT, VI:109; O, 87.

12. For discussion of Kepler's view, see Crombie, "The Mechanistic Hypothesis," 58–59; and Lindberg, *Theories of Vision*, 203.

13. Actually, Descartes does not explicitly state, to my knowledge, what element the animal spirits are, and different commentators interpret them differently. Kemp Smith takes them to be first element, citing several passages in support of this in *New Studies in the Philosophy* (131 and footnote). Others, for example, Maull (265) take them to be third element. The former interpretation seems to me to fit better since the most subtle of the animal spirits are what gives heat to the animate body and thus are like first element particles.

14. *Dioptrics*, AT, VI:111; O, 89.

15. Aristotle, *De Generatione Animalium*, 781a21–23, trans. by Arthur Platt, *The Works of Aristotle*, vol. 5.

16. For a useful exposition of the reasons for and against each of these views, see Modrak, 73–76.

17. Aristotle, *De Juventute et Senectute*, 469a10–15, trans. by J. I. Beare, *The Works of Aristotle*, vol. 3.

18. Aristotle, *De Partibus Animalium*, 666a10–36, trans. by William Ogle, *The Works of Aristotle*, vol. 5. Subsequent citations in text are to this edition and designated *DPA* when necessary.

19. This reading is supported by *De Sensu*, 438b5–10, and by Aristotle's belief that dreams occur because movements that remained in the peripheral organs during the day reach the common organ at night and cause us to believe we see or hear objects not actually present (*De Somnis*, 461a24–30, trans. by J. I. Beare, *The Works of Aristotle*, vol. 3).

20. Polyak, for example, speaks of Descartes' physiological work as "speculations" based on the "few positive anatomical facts known to him" and his theories about the animal spirits as "fantastic elaboration." He also says that Descartes' speculations now appear "naive and vacuous" (100–105).

21. See his letter to Mersenne in 1637, AT, I:378.

22. AT, III:49; K, 72.

23. By image, of course, I do not mean a picture we can look at but a representation that preserves certain essential features of the original. In Descartes' case, the pineal gland image is structurally isomorphic with the retinal image. Each retinal point is represented in the pineal gland image—or rather as many retinal points are represented as the number of optic nerves—and spatial relationships between them are preserved.

24. K, 69–70; AT, III:19. A similar argument is presented in *Passions*, Part I, art. 32; AT, XI:353.

25. AT, III:264; K, 86.

26. AT, III:123–24; K, 75.

27. There are some other reasons that support his choice of the pineal gland, such as its mobility or its location relative to major blood vessels, etc. (see AT, III:263–64; K, 85–86), but these reasons are of less philosophical interest.

28. *Dioptrics*, AT, VI:129; O, 100.

29. AT, III:362.

30. *Treatise on Man*, AT, XI:177.

31. *Treatise on Man*, AT, XI:176–77.

32. *Dioptrics*, AT, VI:130; O, 101.

33. AT, III:493; K, 128.

34. Kemp Smith, *New Studies in the Philosophy*, 145–46; Hamelin, 352–53; and Reed, 733.

35. See, e.g., *Passions*, AT, XI:338; CSM, I:333; and *Dioptrics*, AT, VI:113; O, 101.

36. The connection between brain states and sensations is, therefore, simply a brute fact, which he makes no further effort to explain.

37. *Dioptrics*, AT, VI:130–31; O, 101.

38. This is a rather odd way of putting it, as according to Descartes' theory of light there is no light in objects; they merely reflect in various ways the light given off by luminous bodies.

39. *Dioptrics*, AT, VI:134; O, 104.

40. This sort of problem made it difficult for Berkeley in his *New Theory of Vision* to decide whether magnitude is immediately seen or not.

41. One could, of course, suppose some processes occurring between the retina and the pineal gland that enlarge some parts of the retinal image and diminish others, but it is hard to envision any sort of purely *mechanical* process that could do this in such a way as to produce the observed results.

42. Recent research has shown in a particularly dramatic manner that the colors we see are not determined by the wave length of light hitting the retina. See, e.g., the famous experiment by Land in which subjects saw a fully colored scene even though all the light hitting the eye was in the yellow portion of the spectrum.

43. The function of the visual system, thus understood, is rather similar to that of a device now available for use by the blind called an opticon. It is held in the hand, pressed against a finger, and moved along a line of print. Wherever it encounters black ink, it is activated to produce a vibrating motion against the finger, enabling the person to feel the pattern of the letters. The visual system, of course, is sensitive to a variety of colors and not just black and white, but otherwise the body-machine can be seen as performing the same function as an opticon. God, however, has joined our mind to our body in such a way that the motions transmitted by the optic nerves to the brain cause us to experience sensations of color.

44. See Pirenne, 193–96. He says, among other things, that "there is no neurological explanation of the fact that we normally do not 'see double' when we look at objects with both eyes." Indeed, as he points out, the disparity between the retinal images serves as an important cue for depth perception.

45. This point is often missed by commentators who emphasize the idea that Descartes understands perception in terms of representation rather than resemblance. For while my sensation of, say, blue, does not resemble the motions that cause it, vision occurs by means of an image (pattern of motions) at the surface of the pineal gland, and this image is structurally isomorphic with the retinal image, which in turn does resemble objects (albeit imperfectly). Structural isomorphism is, after all, a kind of resemblance.

46. For a discussion of the way Descartes' theory of vision influenced these philosophers, see my unpublished dissertation, "The Retreat from Realism: Philosophical Theories of Vision from Descartes to Berkeley," Univ. of Wisconsin, Madison, 1984.

47. Descartes' ideas about the role of the animal spirits, for example, were not widely accepted.

4. Descartes' Theory of Visual Spatial Perception

1. See, e.g., the works of Arbini, MacKenzie, and Wilson.

2. Galen, for example, complains that Aristotle failed to explain "how we distinguish the position or size or distance of the perceived object" (cited in Lindberg, "The Science of Optics," 364).

3. He also relies upon the work done by perspectivists on the apparent location of objects seen through lenses or in mirrors in his discussion of the errors of sight.

4. He does, however, use the term *judge* in his discussion of the way in which the blind man with two sticks perceives the situation and says that this case is analogous to visual perception of the situation. This analogy is discussed further in this chapter.

5. See, e.g., Polyak, 103.

6. *Treatise on Man*, AT, XI, Advertisement, vi–vii.

7. Descartes' definition of *situation* is "the direction in which each part of the object lies, with respect to our body" (*Dioptrics*, AT, VI:134; O, 104).

8. *Dioptrics*, AT, VI:134–35; O, 104–5.

9. *Treatise on Man*, AT, XI:159.

10. *Dioptrics*, AT, VI:135; O, 104–5.

11. Berkeley, *Essay*, sec. 89–90. He speaks of the mind "tracing the ray that strikes on the lower part of the eye and being directed to the upper part of the objects," "pursuing the impulses they give in right lines," "hunting for the object along the axes of the radious pencils," etc. (207–8).

12. *Dioptrics*, AT, VI:109; O, 87. In the same vein, he says in Discourse VI that "the soul does not see immediately except by means of the brain (AT, VI:141; O, 108).

13. AT, III:123–24; K, 75.

14. *Dioptrics*, AT, VI:137; O, 105–6.

15. Thomas Reid was the first to make this point, as Daniels argues in *Thomas Reid's Inquiry*. Angell also argues this persuasively in "The Geometry of Visibles."

16. *Dioptrics*, AT, VI:137; O, 106.

17. *Treatise on Man*, AT, XI:160.

18. *Dioptrics*, AT, VI:138; O, 106.

19. See Berkeley, *Essay*, sec. 5, where he says, "There appears a very necessary connection between an obtuse angle and near distance, and an acute angle and farther distance. It does not in the least depend upon experience, but may be evidently known by anyone before he had experienced it." See also Berkeley, *Principles*, sec. 43.

20. See *Treatise on Man*, AT, XI:162–63; and the *Dioptrics*, AT, VI:144–47; O, 108–13.

21. Maull, 254.

22. *Dioptrics*, AT, VI:138; O, 106–7.

23. *Dioptrics*, AT, VI:130; O, 101.

24. *Dioptrics*, AT, VI:138–40; CSM, I:172.

25. *Treatise on Man*, AT, XI:159.

26. *Dioptrics*, AT, VI:140–41; O, 107.

27. *Treatise on Man*, AT, XI:160.

28. *Dioptrics*, AT, VI:140; O, 107.

29. Although when discussing perceptual errors, Descartes conceded that situation perception includes at least a minimal level of judgment (*Dioptrics*, AT, VI:142; O, 108–10).

30. This view is not unchallenged. For example, see Cottingham's article "A Brute to the Brutes?" and Radner and Radner, chap. 1–4.

31. On this point, see also Wilson, "Descartes on the Perception of Primary Qualities," 16.

32. AT, I:378.

33. See, e.g., Cottingham in "A Brute to the Brutes?" where he cites passages where Descartes attributes feelings like hope, fear, and joy to animals. See *Dioptrics*, AT, IV:574; K, 207.

34. See, e.g., Radner and Radner, especially chap. 2 and 3.

35. Perhaps along the lines suggested by MacKenzie, whose interesting rational reconstruction of the *Dioptrics* in "Descartes on Sensory Representation" (127–41) is more consistently mechanistic than Descartes himself.

36. Aristotle himself attributed this ability to the common sense, which integrates the reports of the various senses and checks them against each other, thus correcting this sort of error (*De Somnis*, chap. 3, especially 461b3–8). Although the mechanism by which this is done remains obscure, the important thing for the Aristotelian is that it is done by a *sense* faculty and is not a function of the intellect.

37. Sixth Replies, AT, VII:437; CSM, II:294.

38. Sixth Replies, AT, VII:437–38; CSM, II:295.

39. Sixth Replies, AT, VII:437–38; CSM, II:295.

40. Sixth Replies, AT, VII:438; CSM, II:295.

41. Locke, *Essay*, II. ix. 8.

42. At least in the case of size, shape, and distance perception. The phrase cited about how we make "judgments or even rational inferences" indicates that not all the judgments involved at the third level of sensation involve actual rational calculation. But clearly some do.

43. Hatfield and Epstein attribute this view to Descartes in their article "The Sensory Core and the Medieval Foundations of Early Modern Perceptual Theory," but do not distinguish clearly enough between his position in the *Dioptrics* and that presented in the Sixth Replies.

44. Sixth Replies, AT, VII:437–38; CSM, II:295.
45. See footnote 16 in Introduction for references on this.

Conclusion

1. It must be noted, of course, that Descartes was not the only person working on a mechanistic theory of color, but his work was particularly influential because it was persuasively written and was accessible to popular audiences.

2. This is not to say that there are no dualistic tendencies in Aristotle or that there are no aspects of his theory that might generate this more characteristically modern form of skepticism. His doctrine about the role of phantasms in perception, for example, might do so if pushed in certain directions.

3. Thus Malebranche, for example, supposes that we would see the sides of a cube seen in projection as unequal unless some sort of judgment intervened (*Recherche de la Vérité*, Rodis-Lewis edition, vol. 1, 96), and Locke supposes that when we look at a sphere, the idea imprinted on our mind is that of a "flat circle, variously shaded" (*Essay*, II. ix. 8).

4. Their great interest in what the visual experience of a man born blind who later regained his sight would be like, was due to the hope that this would clarify the nature of what is immediately given in vision, but the results of the first few cases were disappointingly difficult to interpret.

5. He does not actually *say* that a second projection of the retinal image to the pineal gland occurs in sheep, and the figure in question does not show the second projection. But since sheep have pineal glands and presumably do not see double, it seems very likely he thought that this second projection occurs in sheep also.

6. See, e.g., the passage in Aquinas' *Commentary on Aristotle's De Sensu* where he says "sedentary animals do have a certain knowledge of things necessary for them, insofar as they are aware that such are being offered to them here and now; but progressive animals receive knowledge of them even though they are somewhat removed therefrom; hence this more closely approximates intellectual cognition" (Lesson II, n. 23).

7. Again, this is not to say that there are *no* problems within the Aristotelian/Thomistic tradition. There are, for example, problems with the way in which the rational soul and its sensitive and nutritive powers are connected (Descartes points out some of these in his letter to Plempius for Fromondus [AT, I:414–15; K, 36–37]), but the problems are at least *different* ones from those Descartes faces.

8. AT, I:154.
9. AT, I:414; K, 37.
10. AT, III:372; K, 102.
11. See, e.g., the letter where he ascribes feelings of joy, hope, and fear to a bird (AT, IV:574–75; K, 207), or his letter to More where he says that he does not regard it as proved that there is no thought (*cogitationem*) in animals, "since the human mind does not reach into their hearts" (AT, V:276–77; K, 244).
12. AT, V:276.
13. AT, IV:573; K, 206.
14. See, e.g., the attempted rational reconstructions offered by MacKenzie in "Descartes on Sensory Representation" and by Radner and Radner.
15. For one thing, allowing that animals possess thought (*cogitationem* or *pensée*) would, for Descartes, imply that they had immortal souls (AT, IV:576; K, 208).
16. Indeed, if the image is optically stabilized, vision fades away after a few seconds. See Gregory, 44.

BIBLIOGRAPHY

Alquié, Ferdinand. *Descartes: l'Homme et l'Oeuvre*. Paris: Hatier-Boivin, 1956.

Angell, R. B. "The Geometry of Visibles." *Nous* 8 (1974): 87–117.

Anton, John P. *Aristotle's Theory of Contrariety*. New York: The Humanities Press, 1957.

Aquinas, Thomas. *In Aristotelis libros De Sens et Sensato*. Taurini: Marietti, 1928.

———. *Questiones Quodlibetates*. Ed. by R. Spiazzi. Taurini: Marietti, 1949.

———. *St. Thomas Aquinas' Commentary on the Book Concerning the Sensitive Power and the Sensible Thing*. Trans. by Joseph Smolar. In-house translation of *In Aristotelis libros De Sens et Sensato* from the Dominican House of Studies Library in Washington, D.C., 1964.

———. *Summa Contra Gentiles*. Trans. by English Dominican Fathers. London: Burns, Oates & Washbourne, 1923.

———. *Summa Theologica*. Trans. by Fathers of the English Dominican Province. New York: Benziger, 1920.

———. *Truth*. Trans. by Robert Mulligan, Chicago: Henry Regnery, 1952.

Arbini, Ronald. "Did Descartes Have a Philosophical Theory of Sense Perception?" *Journal of the History of Philosophy* 21 (1983): 317–37.

Ariew, Roger. "Descartes and Scholasticism: The Intellectual Background to Descartes' Thought." In *Cambridge Companion to Descartes*, ed. by John Cottingham. Cambridge: Cambridge Univ. Press, forthcoming.

———. "Early 17th Century Philosophy at Paris and the Jesuit Colleges," unpublished manuscript.

Aristotle. *Aristotle's De Anima in the Version of William of Moerbecke and the Commentary of St. Thomas Aquinas*. Ed. by Kenelm Foster and Sylvester Humphries. New Haven: Yale Univ. Press, 1954.

———. *The Works of Aristotle*. Ed. by W. D. Ross. 12 vols. Oxford: Clarendon, 1931.

Beare, John I. *Greek Theories of Elementary Cognition*. Oxford: Clarendon, 1906.

Beck, Leslie John. *The Metaphysics of Descartes: A Study of the Meditations*. Oxford: Clarendon, 1952.

———. *The Method of Descartes: A Study of the Regulae*. Oxford: Clarendon, 1952.

Berkeley, George. *Essay Towards a New Theory of Vision*. Ed. by A. A. Luce. London: Thomas Nelson & Sons, 1967.

———. *Principles of Human Knowledge*. In *Berkeley's Philosophical Writings*, ed. by David Armstrong. London: Collier Books, 1965.

Blackwell, Richard. "Descartes' Laws of Motion." *Isis* 57 (1966): 220–34.

Brockliss, L. W. B. "Aristotle, Descartes and the New Science: Natural Philosophy at the University of Paris 1600–1740." *Annals of Science* 38 (1981): 33–69.

———. *French Higher Education in the Seventeenth and Eighteenth Centuries: A Cultural History*. Oxford: Clarendon, 1987.

Bundy, Murray. "The Theory of Imagination in Classical and Medieval Thought." *University of Illinois Studies in Language and Literature* 12 (1924): 1–289.

Burtt, E. A. *The Metaphysical Foundations of Modern Science*. Rev. ed. New York: Doubleday, 1954.

Carriero, John. "The Second Meditation and the Essence of the Mind." In *Essays on Descartes' Meditations*, ed. by Amelie Rorty, 199–222.

Clarke, Desmond. *Descartes' Philosophy of Science*. Manchester: Manchester Univ. Press, 1982.

Clatterbaugh, Kenneth C. "Descartes' Causal Likeness Principle." *Philosophical Review* 89 (1980): 379–402.

Collins, James. *Descartes' Philosophy of Nature*. American Philosophical Quarterly Monograph, no. 5. Oxford: Blackwell, 1971.

Cook, Monte. "Descartes' Alleged Representationalism." *History of Philosophy Quarterly* 4 (1987): 179–93.

Cottingham, John. "A Brute to the Brutes?: Descartes' Treatment of Animals." *Philosophy* 53 (1978): 551–59.

———. *Descartes*. New York: Basil Blackwell, 1986.

———. "Descartes on Colour." *Proceedings of the Aristotelian Society* 90 (1989–90): 231–46.

Crombie, A. C. "The Mechanistic Hypothesis and the Scientific Study of Vision: Some Optical Ideas as a Background to the Invention of the Microscope." In *Historical Aspects of Microscopy*, ed. by S. Bradbury and G. Turner. Cambridge: Royal Microsophical Society, Heffer & Sons, 1967.

Da Corte, Marcel. "Notes Exégétiques sur la Théorie Aristotelienne du Sensus Communis." *New Scholasticism* 6 (1932): 187–214.

Dalbiez, R. "Les Sources Scholastiques de la Théorie Cartésienne de l'Etre Objective." *Revue de l'Histoire de la Philosophie* 3 (1929): 464–72.

Daniels, Norman. *Thomas Reid's Inquiry: The Geometry of Visibles and the Case for Realism*. Stanford: Stanford Univ. Press, 1989.

Descartes, René. *Descartes' Philosophical Letters*. Trans. by Anthony Kenny. Oxford: Clarendon, 1970.

———. *Descartes' Rules for Direction of the Mind*. Trans. by Lawrence J. La Fleur. New York: Bobbs-Merrill, Liberal Arts Press, 1961.

———. *Discours de la méthode: Texte et commentaire*. Ed. and annotated by Étienne Gilson. Paris: Librairie Philosophique, J. Vrin, 1928.

———. *Discourse on Method, Optics, Geometry and Meteorology*. Trans. by Paul Olscamp. New York: Bobbs-Merrill, 1965.

———. *Oeuvres de Descartes*. Ed. by Charles Adam and Paul Tannery, Rev. ed. 12 vols. Paris: Librairie Philosophique, J. Vrin/C.N.R.S., 1964–76.

———. *Oeuvres philosophiques*. Ed. with annotations by Ferdinand Alquié. 3 vols. Paris: Classiques Garnier, Editions Garnier Frères, 1967.

———. *Philosophical Works of Descartes*. Trans. by Elizabeth Haldane and G. R. T. Ross. 2 vols. Cambridge: Cambridge Univ. Press, 1973.

———. *Philosophical Writings of Descartes*. Trans. by John Cottingham, Robert Stroothoff, and Dugald Murdoch. 2 vols. Cambridge: Cambridge Univ. Press, 1985.

Dijksterhuis, Eduard J. *The Mechanization of the World Picture*. Oxford: Clarendon, 1961.

Doney, Wills, ed. *Descartes: A Collection of Critical Essays*. Garden City, N.J.: Doubleday Anchor Books, 1967.

Duhem, Pierre. *The Evolution of Mechanics*. Germantown, Md.: Sijthoff & Noordhoff, 1980.

Dupleix, Scipion. *Corps de Philosophie, Book VIII, Livre de la physique, ou science naturelle, contenant la cognoissance de l'âme.* Rouen, chez Louis Mesnil, 1640.

Eastwood, Bruce. 1984. "Descartes on Refraction: Scientific vs. Rhetorical Method." *Isis* 75 (1984): 481–502.

Eustace of St. Paul [Eustachio a S. Paulo]. *Summa Philosophiae Quadripartita de rebus Dialecticis, Ethicis, Physicis et metaphysicis.* Cantabrigiae, England, 1640.

Faye, Emmanuel. "Le corps de philosophie de Scipion Dupleix et l'arbre cartésien des sciences." *Corpus* (1986): 7–15.

Galison, Peter. "Descartes' Comparisons: From the Invisible to the Visible." *Isis* 75 (1984): 311–26.

Garber, Daniel. "Descartes, the Aristoteleans and the Revolution That Did Not Happen in 1637." *Monist* 71 (1988): 471–87.

———. "Science and Certainty in Descartes." In *Descartes: Critical and Interpretive Essays,* ed. by Michael Hooker, 114–51.

———. "Semel in Vita: The Scientific Background to Descartes Meditations." In *Essays on Descartes' Meditations,* ed. by Amelie Rorty, 81–116.

Gaukroger, Stephen, ed. "Descartes' Project for a Mathematical Physics." In *Descartes: Philosophy, Mathematics and Physics,* 97–135. Sussex: Harvester, 1980.

Georges-Berthier, Aug. "Le Méchanisme Cartésien et la Physiologie au XVII Siècle." *Isis* 1 (1914): 37–89.

Gibson, James J. *The Senses Considered as Perceptual Systems.* Boston: Houghton Mifflin, 1966.

Gilson, Étienne. "Descartes et la Metaphysique Scholastique." *Revue de l'Université de Bruxelles* (1924): 105–39.

———. *Études sur le Rôle de la Pensée Médiévale dans la Formation du Système Cartésien.* Paris: Librairie Philosophique, J. Vrin, 1930.

———. *Index Scholastico-Cartésien.* Paris: Librairie Philosophique, J. Vrin, 1979.

———. "Recherches sur la Formation du Système Cartésien." *Revue de l'Histoire de la Philosophie* 3 (1929): 113–64.

Goddu, Andre. Review of *Descartes' Theory of Light and Refraction,* by Mark Smith. *Isis* 81 (1990): 107–8.

Gregory, R. L. *Eye and Brain: The Psychology of Seeing.* New York: McGraw-Hill, 1966.

Grene, Marjorie. *Descartes.* Minneapolis: Univ. of Minnesota Press, 1985.

Grontkowski, Christine, and Evelyn Fox Keller. "The Mind's Eye." In *Discovering Reality,* ed. by Sandra Harding and Merrill Hintikka, 207–24.

Hamelin, Oscar. *Le Système de Descartes.* Paris: Librarie Félix Alcan, 1921.

Harding, Sandra, and Merrill Hintikka. *Discovering Reality.* Holland: Reidel, Kluwer Academic Publishing, 1983.

Hatfield, Gary. "Descartes' Physiology and Its Relation to His Psychology." In *Cambridge Companion to Descartes,* ed. by John Cottingham. Cambridge: Cambridge Univ. Press, forthcoming.

———. "The Senses and the Fleshless Eye." In *Essays on Descartes' Meditations,* ed. by Amelie O. Rorty, 49–78.

Hatfield, Gary, and William Epstein. "The Sensory Core and the Medieval Foundations of Early Modern Perceptual Theory." *Isis* 70 (1979): 363–84.

Hayen, André. *L'Intentionnel selon Saint Thomas.* Paris: Desclée de Brouwer, 1954.

Hooker, Michael, ed. *Descartes: Critical and Interpretive Essays.* Baltimore: Johns Hopkins Univ. Press, 1978.

Hymen, John. "The Cartesian Theory of Vision." *Ratio* 28 (1986): 149–67.

John of St. Thomas. *Cursus Philosophicus Thomisticus*. 3 vols. Taurini [Italia] ex officina domus editorialis Marietti, nunc Marii E. Marietti, 1930–37.

Jolley, Nicholas. "Descartes and the Action of Body on Mind." *Studia Leibnitiana*, Band 19, Heft 1 (1987): 41–53.

Kahn, Charles. "Sensation and Consciousness in Aristotle's Psychology." *Archive für Geschicte der Philosophie* 48 (1966): 43–81.

Keeling, S. V. 1937. "Le Réalisme de Descartes et le Rôle des Natures Simples." *Revue de Metaphysique et de Morale* 44 (1937): 63–99.

Kenny, Anthony. *Descartes: A Study of His Philosophy*. New York: Random House, 1968.

———. "The Homunculus Fallacy." In *Interpretations of Life and Mind*, ed. by Marjorie Grene, 66–74. New York: Humanities Press, 1971.

Kessler, Eckhard. "The Intellective Soul." In *Cambridge History of Renaissance Philosophy*, ed. by Charles Schmitt, 485–534.

Klubertanz, George, S. J. *The Discursive Power: Sources and Doctrines of the vis cognitiva According to St. Thomas Aquinas*. St. Louis: The Modern Schoolman, 1952.

Land, E. H. "Experiments in Color Vision." *Scientific American* 200, 1959, 84–94.

Larmore, Charles. "Descartes' Empirical Epistemology." In *Descartes: Philosophy, Mathematics & Physics*, ed. by Stephen Gaukroger, 6–20.

Ledvina, Jerome. *A Philosophy and Psychology of Sensation, With Special Reference to Vision, According to the Principles of St. Thomas Aquinas*. Washington: Catholic Univ. of America Press, 1941.

Lennon, Thomas M. "Representationalism, Judgment and the Perception of Distance: Further to Yolton and McRae." *Dialogue* 19 (1980): 151–62.

Lindberg, David, trans. *On the Multiplication of Species*. In *Roger Bacon's Philosophy of Nature: A Critical Edition*, ed. by Lindberg. Oxford: Clarendon, 1983.

———. "The Science of Optics." In his *Science in the Middle Ages*, 338–68. Chicago: Univ. of Chicago Press, 1978.

———. *Theories of Vision from Al-Kindi to Kepler*. Chicago: Univ. of Chicago Press, 1976.

Locke, John. *An Essay Concerning Human Understanding*. New York: Dover, 1959.

MacKenzie, Ann Wilbur. "Descartes on Life and Sense." *Canadian Journal of Philosophy* 19 (1989): 163–92.

———. "Descartes on Sensory Representation: A Study of the *Dioptrics*." *Canadian Journal of Philosophy* 16 (1990): 109–47.

McRae, Robert F. "Idea as a Philosophical Term in the Seventeenth Century." *Journal of the History of Ideas* 26 (1965): 175–90.

———. "On Being Present to the Mind: A Reply." *Dialogue* 14 (1975): 664–66.

Malebranche, Nicolas. *Recherche de la vérité*. Ed. by Rodis-Lewis. 3 vols. Paris: J. Vrin, 1964.

Marion, Jean-Luc. *Sur la théologie blanche de Descartes*. Paris: Librairie Philosophique, J. Vrin, 1975.

———. *Sur l'ontologie grise de Descartes: Science Cartésienne et Savoir Aristotelicien dans les Regulae*. Paris: Librairie Philosophique, J. Vrin, 1975.

Maull, Nancy L. "Cartesian Optics and the Geometrization of Nature." *Review of Metaphysics* 32 (1978): 253–76.

Mercer, Christia. "The Vitality and Importance of Early Modern Aristotelianism." In anthology ed. by Tom Sorell. Oxford: Oxford Univ. Press, forthcoming.

Mesnard, Pierre. "L'Esprit de la Physiologie Cartésienne." *Archives de Philosophie* 13 (1937): 181–220.

Miles, Murray. "Descartes' Mechanism and the Medieval Doctrine of Causes, Qualities and Forms." *The Modern Schoolman* 65 (1988): 97–116.

———. "The Idea of Extension: Innate or Adventitious? On R. F. McRae's Interpretation of Descartes." *Dialogue* 27 (1988): 15–22.

Milhaud, Gaston. *Descartes Savant*. Paris: Librairie Félix Alcan, 1921.

Modrak, Deborah. *Aristotle: The Power of Perception*. Chicago: Univ. of Chicago Press, 1987.

Mouy, Paul. *Le Development de la Physique Cartésienne*. Paris: Librairie Philosophique, J. Vrin, 1934.

Nathorp, P. "La pensée de Descartes depuis les Regulae jusq'aux Meditations." *Revue de Metaphysique et de Morale* 4 (1986): 416–32.

Novitski, Mary E. "The Empiricism of Descartes' Method." Master's thesis, Univ. of California, Berkeley, 1968.

O'Neil, Brian. "Direct Realism and Sensory Abstraction." *Proceedings of New Mexico-West Texas Philosophical Society* (1974).

———. *Epistemological Direct Realism in Descartes' Philosophy*. Albuquerque: Univ. of New Mexico Press, 1974.

Park, Katharine. "The Organic Soul." In *Cambridge History of Renaissance Philosophy*, ed. by Charles Schmitt, 464–84.

Pastore, Nicholas. *Selective History of Theories of Visual Perception*. New York: Oxford Univ. Press, 1971.

Peifer, John Frederick. *The Concept in Thomism*. New York: Record, 1952.

Pirenne, Maurice Henri Leonard. *Vision and the Eye*. 2d ed. London: Chapman and Hall, 1967.

Pitte, Frederick Van De. "Descartes' Epistemological Revolution: A Modern Realist Transformation of the Doctrine of Forms." *Proceedings of the American Catholic Philosophical Association* 90 (1985): 132–48.

Polyak, Stephen. *The Vertebrate Visual System*. Ed. by H. Kluver. Chicago: Univ. of Chicago Press, 1957.

Popkin, Richard. "Theories of Knowledge." In *Cambridge History of Renaissance Philosophy*, ed. by Charles Schmitt, 668–84.

Prendergast, Thomas. "Motion, Action and Tendency in Descartes' Physics." *Journal of the History of Philosophy* 13 (1975): 453–62.

Pucelle, Jean. "La Théorie de la Perception Extérieure Chez Descartes." *Revue de l'Histoire de la Philosophie* 3 (1935): 297–339.

Radner, Daisie, and Michael Radner. *Animal Consciousness*. Buffalo, N.Y.: Prometheus Books, 1989.

Randall, John Herman. *Aristotle*. New York: Columbia Univ. Press, 1960.

Reed, Edward S. "Descartes' Corporeal Ideas Hypothesis and the Origin of Scientific Psychology." *Review of Metaphysics* 35 (1982): 731–52.

Regis, L. M., O.P. *Epistemology*. New York: Macmillan, 1959.

Reif, Patricia. "The Textbook Tradition in Natural Philosophy, 1600–1650." *Journal of the History of Ideas* 30 (1969): 17–32.

Remnant, Peter. "Descartes: Body and Soul." *Canadian Jounal of Philosophy* 9 (1979): 377–86.

Rochemonteix, Camille de. *Un collége des Jesuites au xviie et xviii siècle: le collège Henri IV de la Flèche*, 4 vols. le Mans, 1889.

Rodis-Lewis, Geneviève. "Limitations of the Mechanical Model in the Cartesian Conception of the Organism." In *Descartes: Critical and Interpretive Essays*, ed. by Michael Hooker, 152–70.

Ronchi, Vasco. *The Nature of Light*. Trans. by V. Barocas. London: Heinemann, 1970.

Rorty, Amelie O., ed. *Essays on Descartes Meditations*. Berkeley: Univ. of California Press, 1986.

Rorty, Richard. *Philosophy and the Mirror of Nature*. Princeton: Princeton Univ. Press, 1986.

Ross, David. *Aristotle*. New York: Barnes and Noble, 1964.

Roy, Jean. *L'Imagination selon Descartes*. 6th ed. Paris: Gallimard, 1944.

Ruvio, Antonio. *Commentaria in Libros Aristoteles De Anima*. Lyon: 1620.

Sabra, A. I. *Theories of Light from Descartes to Newton*. London: Oldbourne, 1967.

Schmitt, Charles. "The Rise of the Philosophical Textbook." In *Cambridge History of Renaissance Philosophy*, 792–803.

——, ed. *Cambridge History of Renaissance Philosophy*. Cambridge: Cambridge Univ. Press, 1988.

Schute, Clarence. *The Psychology of Aristotle: An Analysis of the Living Being*. New York: Russell & Russell, 1964.

Schwarz, H. "Les Recherches de Descartes sur la Connaissance du Monde Extérieur." *Revue de Metaphysique et de Morale* 91 (1986): 459–77.

Scott, Joseph Frederick. *The Scientific Work of René Descartes*. London: Taylor & Francis, 1952.

Signoret, E. "Cartésianisme et Aristotelisme." *Revue de Metaphysique et de Morale* 44 (1937): 287–304.

Sirven, J. *Les années d'apprentissage de Descartes: 1596–1628*. Paris: Librairie Philosophique, J. Vrin, 1928.

Slakey, Thomas. "Aristotle on Perception." *Philosophical Review* 70 (1961): 470–84.

Smith, A. Mark. *Descartes' Theory of Light and Refraction: A Discourse on Method*. *Transactions of the American Philosophical Society*, 77, pt. 3 (1987).

——. "Getting the Big Picture in Perspectivist Optics." *Isis* 72 (1981): 568–89.

Smith, Norman Kemp. *New Studies in the Philosophy of Descartes*. London: Macmillan, 1952.

——. *Studies in the Cartesian Philosophy*. New York: Russell & Russell, 1962.

Soffer, Walter. *From Science to Subjectivity: An Interpretation of Descartes' Meditations*. New York: Greenwood, 1987.

Tachau, Katherine. *Vision and Certitude in the Age of Ockham: Optics, Epistemology and the Foundations of Semantics 1250–1345*. Leiden: E. J. Brill, 1988.

Wallace, William, O.P. *Causality and Scientific Explanation*. Ann Arbor: Univ. of Michigan Press, 1974.

——. "The Philosophical Setting of Medieval Science." In *Science in the Middle Ages*, ed. by David Lindberg, 91–119.

——. *The Scientific Methodology of Theodoric of Freiberg*. Fribourg, Switzerland: The University Press, 1959.

——. "Traditional Natural Philosophy." In *Cambridge History of Renaissance Philosophy*, ed. by Charles Schmitt, 201–35.

Watson, Richard A. *The Downfall of Cartesianism: A Study of Epistemological Issues in Late 17th Century Cartesianism*. The Hague: Martinus Nijhoff, 1966.

Wells, Norman. "Material Falsity in Descartes, Arnauld and Suarez." *Journal of the History of Philosophy* 22 (1984): 25–50.

————. "Objective Reality of Ideas in Descartes, Caterus and Suarez." *Journal of the History of Philosophy* 28 (1990): 33–61.

Westfall, Richard. 1962. "Development of Newton's Theory of Color." *Isis* 53 (1962): 339–58.

Williams, Bernard. *Descartes: The Project of Pure Inquiry*. New York: Penguin, 1978.

Wilson, Margaret. "Cartesian Dualism." In *Descartes: Critical and Interpretive Essays*, ed. by Michael Hooker, 197–211.

————. *Descartes*. London: Routledge & Kegan Paul, 1978.

————. "Descartes on the Perception of Primary Qualities." In *René Descartes: Metaphysics and Classification of the Science in 1637*. Collected papers from the San Jose Summer Institute on Early Modern Philosophy, 35-1 to 35-19, 1988. A revised version of this paper will appear in an anthology edited by Steven Voss published by Oxford University Press, and tentatively titled *Essays on the Philosophy and Science of René Descartes*.

Wolf-Devine, Celia. "The Retreat from Realism: Philosophical Theories of Vision from Descartes to Berkeley." Ph.D. diss., Univ. of Wisconsin, Madison, 1984.

Wolfson, Harry Austryn. "The Internal Senses in Latin, Arabic and Hebrew Philosophic Texts." *Harvard Theological Review* 28 (1935): 69–113.

Yolton, John. "Ideas and Knowledge in Seventeenth-Century Philosophy." *Journal of the History of Philosophy* 13 (1975): 145–65.

————. *Locke and the Way of Ideas*. Oxford: Oxford Univ. Press, 1956.

————. "On Being Present to the Mind: A Sketch for the History of an Idea." *Dialogue* 14 (1975): 373–88.

————. *Perceptual Acquaintance from Descartes to Reid*. Minneapolis: Univ. of Minnesota Press, 1984.

INDEX

CELIA WOLF-DEVINE RECEIVED HER B.A. FROM SMITH COLLEGE AND HER Ph.D. from the University of Wisconsin at Madison. She is an assistant professor of philosophy at Stonehill College and has published several articles on abortion and affirmative action. Her main areas of interest are early modern philosophy, philosophy of perception, and philosophy of sex and gender.